The ILLUSTRATED HISTORY *Of*
CARDIFF'S SUBURBS

The ILLUSTRATED HISTORY Of CARDIFF'S SUBURBS

Dennis Morgan

DB PUBLISHING

First published in Great Britain in 2003 by The Breedon Books
Publishing Company Limited, Breedon House, 3 The Parker
Centre, Derby, DE21 4SZ.

This paperback edition published in Great Britain in 2013 by DB
Publishing, an imprint of JMD Media Ltd

ISBN 978-1-78091-294-3

CONTENTS

Acknowledgements

I would like to express my sincere appreciation to everyone who has helped me in the writing of this book. Mr Brynmor Jones and his colleagues in the Local Studies department of the Central Library provided valuable assistance in my quest for original sources and photographs. Several of the flourishing local history societies in Cardiff gave me similar help. Mr Rupert Harding, formerly of Breedon Books, suggested that I should write this book and I would like to express my appreciation to him for his support and advice during its production. I am indebted to Mr Gerald Mitchell who was kind enough to design the introductory map of Cardiff's suburbs. My thanks also go to Mr Dennis Pope, who has processed the selected photographs with his usual professional expertise.

I would like to extend my gratitude to the organisations and people who have provided photographs and maps for this book. Many of them came from the Local Studies Collection in the Cardiff Central Library. Others have appeared previously in the *Cardiff Yesterday* series published by Stewart Williams. Among other contributors are the following:

John F. Andrews, Associated British Ports, AWE, Marjorie Beavis, Peter Best, Nigel Billingham, Cardiff City Council, Jeff Childs, Sue Davies, Wynford Davies, C. Edwards, Ely Archives Project, Ely Hospital Archives, Lionel V. Evans, Sylvia Francis, Ron German, Glamorgan Record Office, T. Herridge, Graham Horton, Howell's School, Brenda Hutchings, Neville James, Barbara Jones, Bryan Jones, Fred Jones, Steve Jones, Christopher Langmaid, Brian Lee, Tommy Letton, Llandaff Cathedral School, Llanishen Local History Society, Don Llewellyn, Ian Morgan, Sarah Morgan, National Assembly for Wales, Geoff North, Pentyrch & District Local History Society, Geoffrey Pritchard, Rhiwbina Garden Village Society, Roath History Society, Richard Shepherd, *South Wales Echo,* H. Tempest Ltd, E. Turner & Sons Ltd, Whitbread Archives, Robert Williams and Stewart Williams.

I would like to thank them all and apologise if I have inadvertently omitted anyone.

Finally, I am as always grateful for the encouragement and practical help given to me by my family. Ian has taken some of the photographs, Kathryn has helped in the preparation of the maps and Val has made useful suggestions while checking the text. Any errors which remain are my responsibility.

INTRODUCTION

Following their conquest of South Wales, the Romans established a fort by the River Taff on the site where Cardiff Castle now stands. The original fort was constructed in wood but, as the region came increasingly under attack from about AD 250, it was rebuilt in stone. Despite an occupation of nearly 350 years, the Romans never established much more than a military base at Cardiff, though evidence has been found of iron manufacturing nearby. After the departure of the Romans, the site was virtually abandoned for the next 700 years but Caer Taf, or 'the Fortress by the River', is usually considered to be the origin of 'Caerdydd', the Welsh name for Cardiff.

A Norman knight, Robert Fitzhamon, conquered Glamorgan towards the end of the 11th century and he built a motte and bailey castle within the decaying Roman walls at Cardiff. The town began to grow around the castle and soon had a population of about 2,000 people, a figure which hardly varied until the 19th century.

Throughout these years Cardiff was just a small town and port but this did not prevent it from having a turbulent history at times. The borough came under attack on several occasions, especially by those Welshmen who resented their conquerors. The most famous of these assaults was that of Owain Glyndwr in 1404 when he virtually destroyed the town. The castle and the surrounding districts also saw conflict in the Civil War, when the Battle of St Fagans was the most important engagement in Wales during the struggle between King and Parliament. The religious strife of the 16th and 17th century also led to bloodshed in the borough, as both Protestant and Catholic martyrs suffered pain and death for their beliefs.

It was not until the arrival of the Industrial Revolution that major changes in the landscape and population of Cardiff took place. The Bute family, whose considerable wealth was mainly derived from their estates in South Wales, made the crucial decision to build the docks. As the worldwide demand for Welsh coal became insatiable, ships from Cardiff exported these 'black diamonds' to every corner of the globe.

As a result the town was transformed and grew more rapidly than anywhere in Britain during the 19th century. The census of 1801 indicates that a mere 1,870 people lived in the borough but a century later the population was nearly 165,000. The *Golden Daily Mail* of 31 December 1900 observed that, if Cardiff were to continue growing at this rate, by the year 2000 it would have a population of 20 million and would be larger than London. Fortunately that did not happen, and since 1900 the number of inhabitants in the city has increased at a similar rate to the rest of the United Kingdom.

To cope with this flood of newcomers there was a desperate need for room to expand. Ramshackle tenements and hovels were built in seedy courts and alleys which became breeding grounds for disease, as Rammell's Public Health Report of 1849 clearly showed. When the course of the Taff was altered in that same year, the reclaimed land was developed for working-class housing. This district was known as Temperance Town, so called because the landowner would allow no pubs to be built in the area. Nowadays the bus station and the Millennium Stadium occupy much of this site and all traces of those early dwellings have disappeared. Adamsdown and Butetown were other areas to be developed, as the docks were built and activity in the port increased. In a sense these were Cardiff's first suburbs though they lay within the existing boundaries of the town.

Once the available land within the borough had been developed, Cardiff began to encroach into the surrounding villages and hamlets that were destined to become its suburbs. In 1875 Canton, Grangetown, Cathays, Roath and Splott were the first districts to be absorbed into the town. The next great expansion came after World War One, when the most important addition was the village of Ely, the green fields of which were needed for new housing. The extension of Cardiff's boundaries has continued since World War Two with the result that villages, which would once have considered themselves remote from their urban neighbour, now form part of the capital of Wales.

Even before the Romans arrived, these future suburbs were occupied by people who made no attempt to inhabit the marshy, inhospitable, low-lying land where the centre of Cardiff would later be built. There is evidence of Neolithic and Bronze Age activity at Radyr, Ely, Cyncoed and St Fagans. The most notable pre-Roman site in the region is the Iron Age fort at Caerau, while not far away the Romans built a villa where Trelai Park now stands.

I have written the history of Cardiff in my book, *The Cardiff Story*, but this publication concentrates on its suburbs, many of which have a fascinating history in their own right. I have tried to incorporate all the areas which now make up the city and to a large extent I have based the work upon its electoral divisions, though I am aware that well-known districts such as Roath and Llanedeyrn are not electoral divisions. I have also had to take into account the fact that the popular conception of a suburb is not always the same as that decreed by officialdom. Many people living in Cardiff do not always distinguish between Canton and Riverside, Penylan and Cyncoed, or Llandaff and Fairwater. So I apologise in advance to those who think they live in a different district from the one I am writing about. The population statistics are estimates undertaken in 1999 by the Cardiff Research Centre.

The amount of detail allocated to each suburb obviously varies. Some have such a rich history that detailed publications have been written about them. Others appear to have a less exciting tale to tell but sometimes research can indicate a more interesting past than might be supposed. I hope this publication will encourage others to discover more about the history of our city.

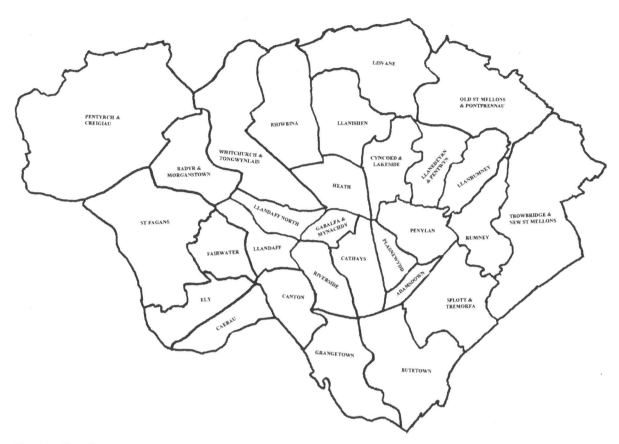

Further Reading:

Davies, J. *A Pocket Guide: Cardiff,* University of Wales Press, 2002.

Morgan, D. *The Cardiff Story,* Dennis Morgan, 2001.

ADAMSDOWN

Population: 8,320

The Cattle Market and the Goods Yard, seen on this map of Adamsdown in 1922, have gone. The modern boundaries of the suburb are bordered by the railway lines to the south and west and Newport Road to the north.

Mediaeval Adamsdown lay just outside the east walls of Cardiff and was owned by the lords of Glamorgan. Traditionally, they allowed the gatekeeper of Cardiff Castle to use the land and the district may take its name from Adam Kyngot, a porter at the castle in 1331.

On the Bute Estate map of 1824, most of the district was occupied by the 270 acres of Adamsdown Farm and the only other building of major significance was Adamsdown House. Set in attactive surroundings, this house was originally the private residence of Henry Hollier, agent to the Marquis of Bute. Later Whitlock Nicholl, a member of a well-known Glamorgan family, lived there and in the 1860s Miss Martha Vaughan purchased the premises to be used as a private girls' school. In the 1870s the house was demolished to make way for Adamsdown Square, by which time the entire suburb was feeling the impact of encroaching urbanisation.

In 1832 a new 'gaol and house of correction' was opened in Adamsdown to replace the former prison in St Mary Street and its 30 cells for men and 25 for women were soon overcrowded. A treadmill, used for pumping water, was worked by male prisoners, while the women did the washing, mended prison clothing or picked oakum. Work on the present building began in 1854 and, as the idea of

rehabilitation replaced that of punishment, other improvements have led to a more humane regime. However, the grim walls of Cardiff Prison remain the most depressing part of the suburb.

As the graveyard of St John's Church in the centre of Cardiff became filled to capacity, the Marquis of Bute provided two acres of land in Adamsdown as a public cemetery in 1848. When an outbreak of cholera swept through the town a year later, the burial ground soon became full and in time degenerated into a public nuisance. The council wanted to convert the site into a recreation ground but, as responsibility lay with the ecclesiastical commissioners, negotiations were protracted and action was not taken until after World War Two. The old cemetery became a park in 1948 but the 19th-century tombstones, many of them with interesting epitaphs, were preserved and re-erected against its stone walls.

Longcross House was built on the site of Payne's Cross, one of the mediaeval boundaries of Cardiff. Following the Chartist Riots, the house was replaced with an army barracks in 1844, which remained in use until 1880.

The land at Longcross was now available for a new hospital and in 1883 the South Wales and Monmouthshire Infirmary was completed at a cost of £23,000. The infirmary was a charity which drew widespread support. Wards were named after wealthy benefactors and Cardiff Corporation made a regular subscription. Workmen from the mines and factories of Glamorgan and Monmouthshire paid into

Miss Vaughan's School for young ladies, c.1870. In the mid-19th century the building was a private residence known as Adamsdown House. The building was demolished a few years after this photograph was taken.

Cardiff Prison, 1951. Knox Road, in the foreground, is named after a governor of the prison and was originally known as Gaol Lane. The houses surrounding the prison were demolished as the area was redeveloped.

Adamsdown Cemetery, 2002. For many years it was an eyesore until the council turned it into a recreation ground. The tombstones along the wall are relics of this early burial ground in Cardiff.

a voluntary scheme at the rate of a penny a week. Contributions also came from the pennies of schoolchildren, the collection made on 'Infirmary Sunday' by the churches and from sporting events or concerts. A sick person did not always find it easy to receive treatment, as he had to find a sponsor from the infirmary's subscribers. Regulations refused admission to, 'persons insane, suffering from an infectious disease or in an incurable state, and women in an advanced stage of pregnancy'. This led to sardonic comments that only the healthy need apply. In 1923 the hospital became the Cardiff Royal Infirmary and continued to give care and treatment to the people of south-east Wales until the end of the 20th century. The closure of the infirmary in 1999 provoked strong protest which has still not abated.

The first part of Adamsdown to be developed was Newtown, where many of the early Irish immigrants settled. By 1855 streets were being built on the meadows of Upper Splott Farm, some of them bearing names drawn from astronomy, such as Star, Planet, Constellation and Eclipse. Other streets are named after metals and precious stones such as Gold, Copper, Topaz, Diamond and Sapphire. Until 30 years ago the Roath Cattle Market and Slaughterhouse were sited near Constellation Street. Older residents of Adamsdown recall how they could not only buy cheaper meat at the slaughterhouse, but also, during World War Two, obtain cuts 'off the ration'. Upper Splott Farmhouse itself was converted into the Great Eastern Hotel in Metal Street, presumably as a tribute to Isambard Kingdom Brunel, whose railway line from Cardiff to London passed through Adamsdown. As the population

The South Wales and Monmouthshire Infirmary, c.1900. Following the death of the King in 1910, it was renamed the King Edward VII Hospital, when a fund was launched in his memory to extend the building and its facilities. Later, the hospital became the Cardiff Royal Infirmary, a name it retained until its closure.

The Great Eastern Hotel was formerly Upper Splott Farmhouse. Now a public house, its name is derived from Brunel's steamship, the Great Eastern, which was launched in 1858 and was the largest steamship of its time.

of the suburb increased, Broadway, known as Green Lane until 1875, and Clifton Street became the principal shopping centres of the district.

A number of fine churches were built in Victorian Adamsdown, though many of them have now been converted to other purposes. The Welsh Calvinistic Methodist Chapel at the corner of Clifton Street is an arts centre and Ebenezer Baptist Chapel in Pearl Street is a Sikh temple. The architecture of St German's in Star Street has been described as 'nothing short of a masterpiece'. This superb Decorated Gothic structure was erected in 1884, when its High Anglicanism represented the 19th-century aspirations of the Oxford Movement to bring the 'beauty of Holiness' to the poorer sections of society.

Cardiff's first municipal secondary school was established at Howard Gardens in 1884. It soon became popular with parents, as it was well equipped and its first headmaster, James Waugh, set high standards. Howard Gardens went on to become one of Cardiff's grammar schools but in March 1941 it suffered severe damage through enemy action and was relocated after the war. Howard Gardens, like Glossop Terrace and Fitzalan Place, takes its name from Lady Gwendoline Howard, the wife of the 3rd Marquis of Bute. The school was built on his land and he also presented the gardens as a recreational park for local people. The Art Department of UWIC (University of Wales Institute Cardiff) now stands on the site of the former school amid fine Victorian Gothic houses.

Adamsdown has had an extensive facelift in recent years. Across the road from the brooding presence of the prison, the magistrates' courts and a public house, appropriately named 'Rumpole's', are both attractive examples of modern architecture. Imaginative housing initiatives at reasonable prices have replaced earlier industrial sites, including the former railway goods depot in Davis Street and the slaughterhouse in Constellation Street. Unfortunately, the splendid Victorian buildings, which once adorned Newport Road from the infirmary to the city centre, were demolished and replaced with tower blocks in the 1960s and 70s. The highest of these is Brunel House at the gateway to the city centre which, as John Newman has put it, 'makes absolutely no concession to its surroundings'.

Howard Gardens, c.1900. The houses are still there though the ivy and the gas lamps, like the school and the gardens on the opposite side of the road, have gone.

Further Reading:

Childs, J. *Roath, Splott and Adamsdown*, Chalford Publishing Company, 1999.

BUTETOWN

Population: 6,120

Butetown was a desolate moor until the 19th century, when the 2nd Marquis of Bute decided to build the first dock in South Wales. At its opening in 1839, the American Consul prophesied that it would bring prosperity to Cardiff 'as long as grass grew and water ran'. Events proved him right, though even the Marquis could not have foreseen the insatiable worldwide demand for Welsh coal in the years to come. He died in 1848 but, during the lifetime of his son, four more docks were built to handle the trade in addition to others at Penarth and Barry.

The Marquis intended Butetown to be a respectable, middle-class suburb, reflecting favourably on him. Fine houses, occupied by sea captains, merchants, stockbrokers and professional people, were built in Mountstuart Square and Loudoun Square. However, as Butetown became overcrowded, noisy and disreputable, wealthier people moved to the leafy suburbs and in their place arose a multi-ethnic community drawn from every corner of the globe. A volatile population of sailors, dockers, labourers, as well as an assortment of shady characters, made Bute Street the most cosmopolitan highway in Britain. Greeks, Arabs and Africans, many of them in national dress, mingled with Italian ice-cream sellers, Chinese

Bute Street, a name familiar to sailors all over the world, c.1920. The Consulate Buildings on the right accommodated the consuls of Belgium, Holland, Russia and Brazil.

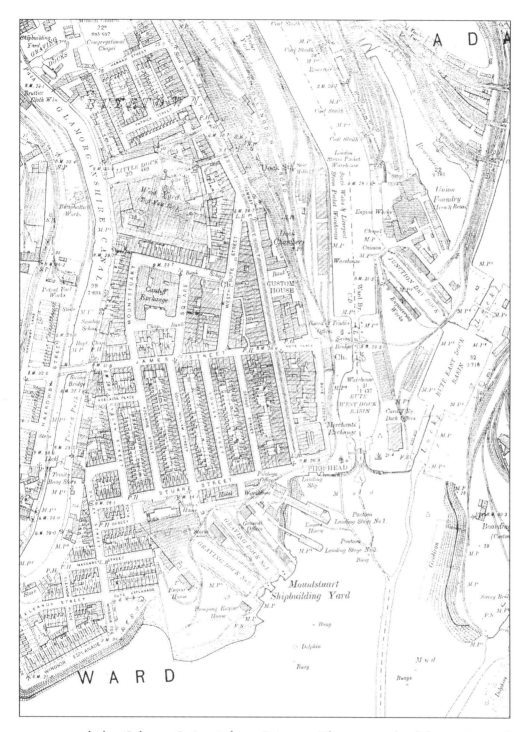

Among the landmarks which have disappeared on this map of Butetown in 1901 are the West Dock, the Glamorganshire Canal and the rows of houses between Stuart Street and James Street. The Exchange was then in its heyday and the Pier Head Building was the headquarters of the dock offices.

seamen and the 'Johnny Onions' from Brittany. The once splendid mansions of Loudoun Square lost their earlier elegance as they were turned into seedy lodging houses or converted into overcrowded tenements for three or four families.

The district below the bridge at Bute Road became known as 'Tiger Bay', possibly from a music hall song of the 1860s. Howard Spring graphically described the Tiger Bay of the early 20th century in *Heaven Lies About Us*: 'Children of the strangest colours, fruits of frightful misalliances, staggered half-naked about the streets ... the

West Bute Street in 1908, when Tiger Bay attracted people from every corner of the globe. The Bute Road Station, the docks terminus of the Taff Vale Railway, is in the background at the centre of the photograph.

flags of all nations flutered on the housefronts ... It was a dirty, smelly, rotten and romantic district, an offence and an inspiration, and I loved it'.

From its earliest days, lurid tales were told about Tiger Bay. In 1856 American and Greek seamen clashed and resorted to the use of knives and revolvers but as an observer noted, 'those encounters were of such frequent occurrence that very little notice was taken of them'. In a seaport as busy as Cardiff, violent incidents and dens of vice were inevitable. One policeman claimed to have raided 80 brothels in a year and no doubt 'ladies of the night' often relieved drunken sailors of their worldly wealth. Some of them might even have woken up next day to find themselves 'shanghaied', on a ship bound for the other side of the world.

Race relations were normally harmonious in Butetown. As one resident recalled, it was the one place where 'a coloured man could call himself a Welshman and get away with it'. A great local character was Tommy Letton, who sold fresh fish from his barrow in the district. In a TV programme he said: 'Everyone knew one another and trusted one another. Doors were never locked and racial discrimination was unheard of'. His readiness to help other people made him a local celebrity and Letton Way is named after this friendly, hardworking man.

However, racial conflict erupted if white people felt their living was under threat from blackleg labour. The seamen's strike of 1911 was particularly vicious, as Chinese laundries and lodging houses were set ablaze and a battalion of the Lancashire Fusiliers was needed to restore order. It was a similar story in 1919, when riots broke out in Tiger Bay and local people were accused of taking jobs from demobilised soldiers.

This unique community has produced its fair share of personalities. The most famous is Shirley Bassey, who was born at Adeline Street in 1937. The youngest of seven children, she began work in a sausage factory but, by the age of 16, she was appearing in working men's clubs. By the time she was 20, Shirley was starring in shows in London, Paris, Monte Carlo and Las Vegas. She went on to sing three title songs for the 'Bond' films, the most famous of which was *Goldfinger*. She was made a Dame Commander in the Millennium New Year's Honours List and later that year topped the bill at the Royal Variety Command Performance. This entertainer, who has enthralled millions around the world, once said she preferred dancing as a youngster and would never have taken up singing had it not been for her mother's persistence.

The falling demand for Welsh coal in the interwar years led to the decline of the docks. In World War Two there was a temporary reprieve, as the ports of South Wales handled 75 percent of American supplies during the build-up to the D-Day landings. A monument in Cardiff Bay to the Welsh merchant seamen who died in the Battle of the Atlantic also serves as a reminder of the sacrifice made by many people in this district during that conflict.

Trade fell away once more after 1945 and coal exports ended in 1964, the year that the West Dock, which had been the foundation of Cardiff's prosperity, was closed. Architectural gems were demolished as Butetown lapsed into decay. Families who had lived in the area for years have still not forgiven the planners for their lack

Tommy Letton not only sold fish in Butetown for 40 years but became a trusted friend to many of his customers.

An aerial view of Cardiff Docks in the 1920s. From the left, at the top are the Bute West Dock, now filled in, and the East Dock. In the centre are the Roath Basin and Roath Dock, and at the bottom is the Queen Alexandra Dock.

Loudoun Square, c.1960. Though these fine houses had lost much of their former elegance, restoration would have been better than demolition.

of vision in the 1960s. Houses, such as those in Loudoun Square with their air of faded grandeur, became a part of history as they were bulldozed and replaced with a featureless modern estate. The film, *Tiger Bay*, starring John and Hayley Mills, was shot on location in 1959 and contains some of the final memories of that colourful district.

The multi-ethnic nature of Butetown has led to a rich variety of religious buildings. St Mary's Church in Bute Street was built on land provided by the 2nd Marquis and, when it was opened on 16 December 1843, he led a procession from the Town Hall as ships in the harbour raised their colours. The earliest Roman Catholic church in Cardiff, dedicated to St David, was opened in Bute Terrace and a Greek Orthodox Church was built near St Mary's in 1906. The first mosque was built in Peel Street but aroused controversy among Muslims amid complaints that it was not properly orientated towards Mecca. In the 1980s it was replaced with the present building in Alice Street. The Norwegian Church was built for the Scandinavian community near the West Dock and has close associations with Roald Dahl and his family. Its flags of the Baltic states, views of the Norwegian fjords and portraits of the Scandinavian royal families led to it being described as the 'cosiest and most beautifully kept seaman's mission in all Britain'. By the 1970s it had been seriously vandalised and was demolished. Fortunately, its memories have been revived with the construction of a new Norwegian Church near the Cardiff Bay Visitors' Centre.

The new Norwegian Church has added to the amenities of Cardiff Bay and has become a popular place for social gatherings and meetings.

The County Hall, built in this interesting 'Pagoda' style, overlooks the former East Dock. Over 1,000 people work there and its opening in 1988 marked an early stage in the rejuvenation of Cardiff Bay.

At the end of the 20th century, the waterfront once again became Cardiff's most dynamic region. Regeneration began in the 1980s, when the council headquarters was established at Atlantic Wharf overlooking the former East Dock. Ambitious plans were to follow, including the construction of the Cardiff Bay Barrage, a freshwater lake stretching from Queen Alexandra Dock to Penarth Head. It has been described as 'a place in which people will want to live, work and play', though critics maintain that it upsets the ecological balance of the bay, while a rise in the level of groundwater poses a threat to property.

New apartments, offices, hotels and restaurants in the bay are interspersed among canals, promenades and the former docks. Old warehouses have been renovated and some of the historic buildings, which managed to survive the architectural carnage of the 1960s, symbolise the great days before 1914 when 'King Coal' dominated this part of the world.

The Pier Head Building has been designated as an information centre for the Welsh Assembly. This magnificent structure was built in 1896 as the offices of the Bute Docks Company. Constructed in red brick and terracotta, it was designed by William Frame, a pupil of William Burges, so it is not surprising that much of the building resembles Burges's work at Cardiff Castle. Their love of Gothic architecture is shown in the magnificent skyline of pinnacled turrets, gargoyles and clustered hexagonal chimneys, all culminating in a splendid castellated clock tower.

The Pier Head Building and the Mermaid Shopping Centre. The old and the new combine to illustrate the transformation of Cardiff Bay in the last 20 years.

The Coal and Shipping Exchange in Mountstuart Square, at present awaiting a new purpose, is another reminder of the docks in their heyday. The docksmen, as shipping and colliery owners were known, used to assemble on its floor before World War One, resplendent in top hat, morning coat, spats and walking cane. Fortunes were made and sometimes lost, as it seemed the demand for Welsh coal would last for ever.

Plans to build a new opera house in Cardiff Bay came to naught but the Millennium Theatre, due to open in 2004, will provide a home for the Welsh National Opera. Not far away at Mermaid Quay, the Roald Dahl Plass is already a popular venue for open-air concerts and theatre. A new chamber for the Welsh Assembly, which at present meets in Crickhowell House, is being built despite concerns about the cost of £55 million.

There is no doubt that the development of Cardiff Bay has given a new lease of life to Butetown. The revitalised docklands have provided 16,000 new jobs, but those who lived there long before this regeneration began feel that not enough of these opportunities have come to them. There could be resentment towards the newcomers who have little in common with the cosmopolitan community that was once Tiger Bay.

The Coal Exchange was opened in 1886 at a cost of £40,000. It was designed by Edwin Seward and this photograph shows the building after its extension was added in 1892.

Further Reading:

Evans, C. and S. Dodsworth, J. Barnett *Below the Bridge,* National Museum of Wales, 1984.

Sinclair, M.C.N. *The Tiger Bay Story* Butetown History & Arts Project, 1993.

Owen, W.R. *Tiger Bay* in Glamorgan Historian Vol. VII 72-86, Stewart Williams, 1970.

CAERAU

Population: 10,780

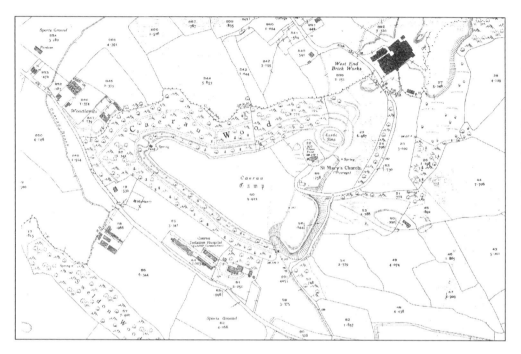

This map of 1940 shows the surroundings of St Mary's Church and the ancient hill fort. Caerau Wood is still a part of the scene today but the isolation hospital and Caerau House, on its right, have gone. Most of this area is now covered with housing.

The history of Caerau and Ely, both of which became part of Cardiff in 1922, is closely interwoven. The modern electoral division shows Caerau lying south of Cowbridge Road West, so that places associated with Ely's history, such as the racecourse and Ely Homes, actually lay in Caerau.

The remains of an Iron Age hill fort overlook the modern housing estate. The site originally covered 12 acres and even today, though much reduced in size, the earthworks remain a formidable testament to the ingenuity of the Silurian warriors who built it. Ditches and ramparts of earth and stone were constructed like the contours of a relief map. Every point of access was heavily fortified with the entrances turned inwards to give a defensive corridor. At the summit, a wooden palisade provided cover for defenders to pepper their foe with a bombardment of stones. For hundreds of years, this stronghold allowed the Silures to control the Taff-Ely Estuary and 1,000 years later the Normans recognised its importance when they built a castle inside the fort.

In 1894 a Roman villa was discovered on Ely Racecourse and excavations were carried out by Sir Mortimer Wheeler in 1922. The results showed a colonnade in front of the house, several outbuildings and a bath suite to the west. Materials for the limestone walls and red pennant roof tiles were obtained from local quarries. To

Some of the earthworks remaining from the Iron Age fort of the Silures. The view across modern Caerau shows how well they chose this defensive position.

ease the discomfort of a cold British winter, coal was used to heat the baths and central heating system. As the land was unsuitable for agriculture, the villa was used to manufacture iron. Coal and iron ore were obtained locally for the smelting process and there is evidence that manganese, imported from Spain, was used to improve the quality of the metal.

Apart from constructing a castle within the Iron Age fort, the Normans also built a stone church. St Mary's is first mentioned in 1291 as part of the deanery of Newport. Built in a Gothic style with a saddle-back roof, the church suffered from vandalism as early as the Reformation, when statues, murals and the rood loft were destroyed. A major restoration was carried out in the 1880s at a cost of £760 but its lonely position has always made the church a target for vandals. By 1957 services had ceased and the building was in a sorry, dilapidated state. A concerted effort was made by local volunteers from all church denominations to restore St Mary's but their work has proved to be in vain. Since the 1970s the church has been a derelict ruin.

Originally attached to the lordship of Llandaff, the manor of Caerau passed through various owners after the Reformation, including the Earl of Pembroke and the Mathew family. In 1861 its population was 131, most of whom were labourers, though the census also reveals that a shepherd, a dressmaker and a woodcutter lived there.

Sir Edward Hill, former MP for Bristol South and managing director of Hill's Dry

Dock in Cardiff, built Caerau House in 1903. This fine building, which unfortunately no longer exists, was set in spacious grounds south of Caerau Wood and St Mary's Church. Its 255 acres included a farm used mainly for breeding horses. Roses and spring bulbs were planted in a wide passage through the woods, 'to complete a fairyland of sheer beauty'.

When Caerau House ceased to be a private residence, it served as living quarters for some of the staff working at the isolation hospital nearby. In 1947 the hospital was adapted to accommodate geriatric patients and later became a hostel. Both Caerau House and the hospital no longer exist and the site is now being developed by the Treharne housing estate, where Barratt's are building 40 private houses.

By 1864 racing at Ely was a regular event and the races that year were acclaimed as 'the most brilliant and successful ever held'. Meetings at the racecourse brought a carnival atmosphere, as the horses were led from Ely Station to the stables at the rear of Mill Road. Jockeys, trainers, over-dressed bookmakers and spectators mingled with jugglers, minstrels and other entertainers, while the police kept a watchful eye for pickpockets. In 1895 the first Welsh Grand National was held and crowds of 40,000 were not uncommon for such an event. Unfortunately, the racecourse never recovered from a fire in 1937 which destroyed the grandstand. The council decided not to renew its lease and in April 1939 the last race to be held there was won by Grasshopper, ridden by Keith Piggott, father of the famous Lester Piggott.

St Mary's Church, c.1940. Its isolated position has made it an easy target for vandals and it is many years since services have been held in the building.

Caerau House in 1979, just before its demolition. When Sir Edward Hill died in 1904, the house was occupied by his son, Vernon, who played cricket for Somerset.

These Victorian buildings of Ely Hospital served first as an industrial school and later as an institution for the mentally ill. Now they have been demolished and replaced with new homes for the people of Cardiff.

The Ely Industrial School was built in 1862 as part of the Cardiff Poor Law Union. Ely Lodge, as it was known, provided education and training for 320 orphan or destitute children who were taught simple trades or prepared for a life in service. In 1908 children needing care were taken out of the workhouse atmosphere and placed in cottage homes around the city. Ely Lodge then became a hospital and in 1948 was given the responsibility of treating patients with psychiatric problems. In 1967 there was a scandal when the Howe Report severely criticised the conditions and care for patients. The report led to more resources becoming available but, as the number of patients declined, the hospital closed in 1999.

Ely Racecourse in its heyday. The horses are parading in front of crowded stands, prior to the Welsh Grand National of 1924.

Among the industries of Caerau were two brickworks giving employment to hundreds of people. Their raw material was the red marl clay from nearby pits. The West End works, not far from St Mary's Church, closed soon after World War Two but the Highland Park factory nearby was still manufacturing more than 300,000 bricks a week shortly before its closure in 1970.

The opening of a servicing depot by the Western Welsh Omnibus Company along Cowbridge Road in 1931 was welcomed at a time of high unemployment. A huge workshop, 300 yards long and 120 yards wide, had space for coachbuilders, fitters, stores, a paint shop and machine shops. It was a major blow when the company moved to Chepstow in 1981 and a supermarket now occupies the site.

In 1939 the Air Ministry purchased 31 acres of land in Caerau Lane to service 24 barrage balloons for the defence of Cardiff. They were sent to various parts of the city to be deployed as a deterrent against low-flying aircraft. It was not unknown for

In 1960 these balloon hangars at Caerau Lane still survived as a memory of the war years. Today the Western Leisure Centre occupies the site.

these monsters to run amok and on one occasion a balloon fell to earth in flames, after it was struck by lightning over Cardiff Castle. Ely Racecourse became a site not only for balloons but also for anti-aircraft guns and a rocket battery.

Not until 1939 were plans put forward to build a major housing estate in Caerau, though patches of development were appearing around Cowbridge Road and Caerau Square. When the war ended, prefabricated houses were erected as an emergency measure to combat the post-war housing shortage and, within a few years, work began on a large housing estate which eventually reached almost to St Mary's Church. Homes and schools sprang up where horses' hooves had once thundered on the old racecourse, though enough of it was preserved to become Trelai Park, the largest complex of playing fields in Cardiff.

Further Reading:

Billingham N. and S.K. Jones *Ely, Caerau and Michaelston-super-Ely* (Chalford Publishing Comlany1996).

CANTON

Population: 13,480

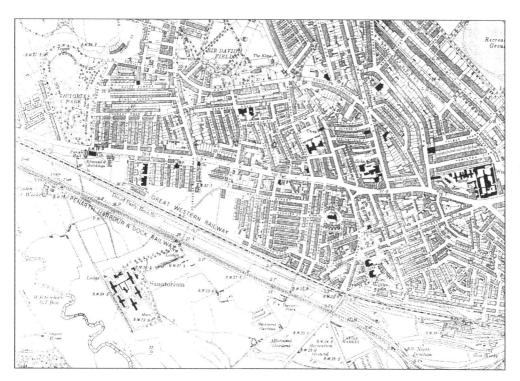

The urbanisation of Canton appears almost complete on this map of 1922. However, since that time, the Victoria Park district and the area south of the railway line, around the Sanatorium and Ninian Park, have also been developed.

A tiny hamlet probably existed in Canton before the arival of the Normans, though written evidence only emerges in the 12th century, when the district became one of the manors owned by the Bishop of Llandaff. Its territory stretched from Llandaff Fields to Leckwith Moors where, until 50 years ago, Romany gypsies pitched their camp. The area was sparsely populated but the bishop owned a mill and a manor house which were sited west of Canton Common, near the junction where Atlas Road and Leckwith Road now meet. In the 16th century the Mathew family purchased the lease from the bishop and held the property until 1818. It was then sold to Sir Samuel Romilly, who disposed of it to William Sheward Cartwright in 1852. The parish was formally incorporated into the borough of Cardiff in 1875. The manor house and Canton Square survived until the early 20th century but, during the next 25 years, the landscape of Canton was largely transformed into the suburb we know today.

The parish church of St John the Evangelist was designed by John Prichard and J.P. Seddon, the architects responsible for the restoration of Llandaff Cathedral. Completed in 1871, its glory lies in the slender, elegant spire, which makes it one of the most attractive churches in Cardiff. One of its chapels is dedicated to St Canna.

She was a sixth-century lady of royal blood who had a beautiful voice and wooed pagans into becoming Christians by singing to them from a bridge at Pontcanna. Canton, or Treganna as it is in Welsh, probably takes its name from her.

Other splendid churches and chapels in Canton represented virtually every denomination of the Christian faith. St Mary's Roman Catholic Church in Kings Road is a large Gothic structure. Conway Road Methodist Church and Capel Salem in Market Road, which the Calvinistic Methodists likened to 'a cathedral of their denomination', are among the many fine Nonconformist chapels.

An indication of Canton's growing commercial importance came with the opening of the Canton Cattle Market and Slaughterhouse in 1859. Fairs were held monthly and by the 1880s, stables, sheds, animal pens and a meat market covered six acres along Market Road from Carmarthen Street to Cowbridge Road. The Market Hotel also stood on the site until it was replaced with the much more splendid Corporation Hotel in 1889. After Canton became a suburb of Cardiff, the council took over the administration of the market. There were some attractive walnut trees within its precincts and local people tried to collect the nuts by throwing stones at the trees. Councillors decided to stop this practice by ordering that the walnuts should be sold as soon as they were ready for picking. Howard Spring recalled the fascination of the slaughterhouse during his childhood. He was 'drawn by the repulsion of its dreadful sights and sounds and smells' and remembered a workman, 'an apparition from Hell', who was generous enough to give the boys a pig's bladder to play football with.

In what must be one of the last rural photographs of Canton, geese are crossing Canton Square in 1890. Atlas Place was later built on this site.

The market has been gone for many years and so has the Atlas Engineering Works in Atlas Terrace. Before World War One the works constructed a range of products, varying from railway wagons to colliery plant and screw propellors. Another major employer was William Vaughan, a local councillor and preacher at Conway Road Methodist Church, who set up his laundry and dry cleaning business in 1860. For more than a century people from all parts of Cardiff brought their laundry and their clothing to be cleaned and pressed at the Llandaff Road premises.

Two of Cardiff's most famous sons came from Canton. Howard Spring was born at 32 Edward Street, later renamed Albert Street, in 1889. He left school at the age of 12 and completed his education by attending night school. Howard began work as a delivery boy and then became a messenger at the *South Wales Echo* before setting out on his journalistic career. Later he found fame as a novelist. Some of his books, such as *Fame is the Spur*, based on the career of Ramsay MacDonald, and *My Son, My Son*, have become classics which have been televised or made into films. One of Spring's works, *Heaven Lies About Us*, is a nostalgic account of his early life and upbringing in Cardiff.

St John's Church soon after its completion in 1871. Previously Llandaff Cathedral had served as the parish church for Canton.

Sir William Goscombe John was another distinguished Cardiffian who grew up in Canton. He was born at 3 Union Street, later known as Gray Street, in 1860 and began his education at the National School in Leckwith Road. Goscombe John was one of the greatest sculptors of his time. The statue of St David in the City Hall and the elegant, equestrian statue of Lord Tredegar in the Gorsedd Gardens are superb examples of his work. Nor was his craft restricted to Wales, as he designed the splendid statue of Lord Salisbury in Westminster Abbey and the regalia for the Investiture of the Prince of Wales in 1911. That same year Goscombe John was deservedly knighted for his services to Welsh culture and in 1936 he was given the freedom of Cardiff.

The National School was the sole provider of education to the children of Canton until 1882. Apart from Goscombe John, Sir Charles Melhuish, who became Lord Mayor of Cardiff, and Sir John Ballinger, who helped to make the Cardiff Library one of the finest in Wales, can be numbered among its pupils. Severn Road was the

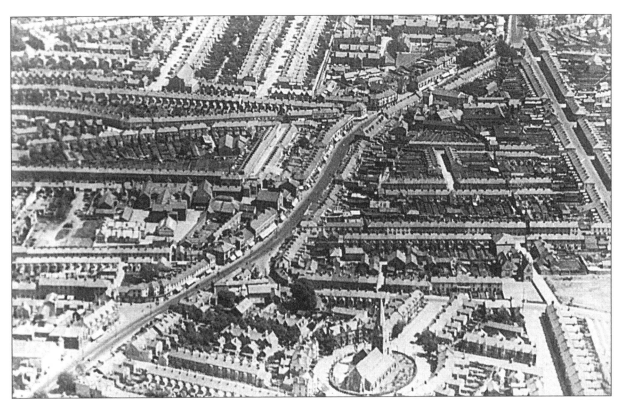

In this aerial view of 1927, Cowbridge Road is weaving a diagonal path through Canton towards Riverside. At the bottom of the photograph, St John's Church stands out just right of centre.

Sir William Goscombe John (right) and the Earl of Plymouth (left) receive the Freedom of the City of Cardiff at the City Hall on 26 October 1936. The work of Goscombe John has won universal acclaim, both within Wales and elsewhere.

first board school to be opened in the district and Howard Spring gives an entertaining account of his schooldays there. Another of Severn's famous pupils was Ernie Curtis who played for the Cardiff City cup winning team of 1927. Radnor Road School can also boast an eminent Welsh footballer, as this was where John Toshack first began to play the game competitively. He won virtually every honour in the game with Liverpool before going into management. Real Madrid, the greatest football club in the world, was among those who employed him in this role.

John also attended Canton High School in Market Road. Originally opened in 1907, the school offered splendid opportunities to youngsters fortunate enough to qualify for a grammar school education. Much of the building was destroyed by enemy action on 2 January 1941 and, though it was repaired after the war, the school moved to new premises at Fairwater in 1963. The Market Road site is now the Chapter Arts Centre.

In 1885 the Cartwright family sold Ely Common and Canton Common to the council for recreational purposes and Canton Common was to provide a home for the Cardiff City Football Club. It was in 1899 at 1 Coldstream Terrace, the home of Bartley Wilson, that the Riverside Football Club was formed. As the team progressed, it changed its name to Cardiff City in 1908. Two years later the club entered the ranks of the professionals and moved to their new stadium at Ninian Park in Sloper Road. At that time the team was a modest Southern League side but after World War One Cardiff City won promotion to the First Division. In 1927 the club enjoyed its greatest moment when it became the first and so far the only team to take the FA Cup out of England.

Victoria Park, on the former Ely Common, was opened at the time of Queen Victoria's Diamond Jubilee in 1897. It was beautifully landscaped with flower beds, a bandstand, a lake and the first public bowling green in Cardiff. Above all, the park is remembered as the home of Billy the seal. He was brought to Cardiff in 1912 on a fishing trawler and the lake at Victoria Park became his home. The public, especially children, loved him and, when food was scarce in World War One, the council decided that, rather than have him destroyed, he should be put on half rations. Frank Hennessy has immortalised Billy in a song which tells of

This plaque is displayed at Barclays Bank in Albert Street as a tribute to Howard Spring. This famous novelist never forgot his roots and in his book, Heaven Lies About Us, *he gave a wonderful portrayal of Cardiff in the early 20th century.*

Ninian Park, soon after it became Cardiff City's stadium in 1910. The ground was named in honour of Lord Ninian Stuart who guaranteed payment of the club's ground rent to the council.

Victoria Park, 1925. The tank on the right is a trophy of World War One and was removed for scrap metal when Britain went to war again in 1939.

his escapades in the flood of 1927 when, according to Frank, he boarded a tram along Cowbridge Road and called in a pub for 'a half of dark'. When Billy died in 1939, it turned out that the much loved seal was in fact a female.

Another attractive open space in Canton is Thompson's Park. Alongside his home at Penhill, Charles Thompson constructed the grounds at his own expense in 1891 and gave the park to the council 20 years later. Thompson's Park is really constructed on two levels. The upper level is a large playing field, leading down through a woodland dell into a park of lovely flower gardens and a pretty pool adorned with what many people believe is Goscombe John's finest creation. The statue he designed for the pool was described by Howard Spring as a 'gracious little boy, sleek and shining as a seal in the water'.

Cowbridge Road has been the main shopping centre of Canton for over a century. One shop, known throughout Cardiff, was Franklyn's Bakery at the corner of Gray Street. Invariably the shop was closed by three in the afternoon as its bread and cakes for the day were all sold. Sadly, Franklyn's has gone, but one family business which still survives can be found near the corner of Albert Street, where Charles Pope opened a photographic and fancy goods shop in 1925. At one time he also ran a lending library from the shop and his son, Dennis, still carries on a personalised photographic service for his customers.

Two popular cinemas in Canton before their closure in the early 1960s were the Coliseum and the Canton. They changed their programmes twice a week and their prices were cheaper than in the city centre. The Coliseum was particularly attractive

Onlookers feed the swans at Thompson's Park before World War One, while the fountain plays around Goscombe John's graceful statue of a little boy.

Cowbridge Road at its junction with Llandaff Road and Leckwith Road in 1909. The forms of transport may be different but most of the buildings in this photograph are still recognisable today.

to children as the projector often broke down and they were allowed to come back the next night to see the rest of the performance.

In 1945 the proposal that George Thomas, later Lord Tonypandy, should become a Labour Party candidate for the constituency was made in Canton at a café near Ninian Park. The great Speaker of the House of Commons retained his seat until his retirement in 1983. He always regarded the Canton Ward as the centre of his constituency and often spoke of his affection for its people. Like everywhere else, Canton has changed since World War Two, but the suburb is still recognisable as that created in the Victorian and Edwardian periods.

Further reading:

Jones, B. *Canton*, Chalfont Publishing Company, 1995.

CATHAYS

Population: 14,650

Cathays Park is world famous as the site of Cardiff's splendid civic centre but the origin of the name is somewhat unclear. 'Hays' signifies hedges or woodland and one possibility is that the district was once inhabited by wild cats. However, from the

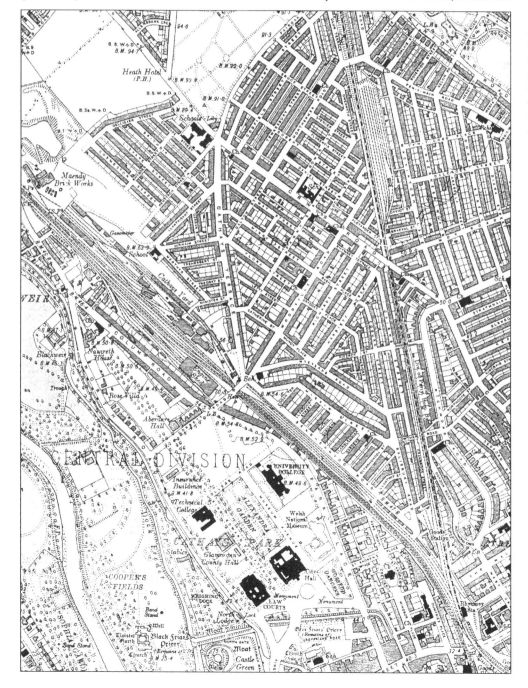

Cathays has changed little since this map of 1922, though there are now more buildings in the Civic Centre and the area around Maindy Brickworks has been developed.

For centuries, the grange was one of the most notable landmarks in Cathays. This photographer, watched by interested onlookers, may be taking a picture for posterity before the grange became a part of history.

Welsh word 'cad', meaning a battle, it is possible that an unknown conflict was fought in Cathays.

The northern limit of mediaeval Cardiff was marked by the cross where Fairoak Road and Crwys Road now meet. At that time Cathays Grange, probably granted by William Doggevel of Roath to Margam Abbey, was the most important building in the area, and until 1899 its thatched, stone farmhouse and barn stood near Cathays Terrace.

In 1766 the 1st Marquis of Bute inherited lands in Cathays through his marriage to Charlotte Windsor. He later purchased other properties in the district including Cathays Park, the cornerstone of his estate in Cardiff. Cathays House, which he built at a cost of £40,000, was expensively landscaped, furnished and decorated. It was demolished by the 2nd Marquis in 1815 who preferred to use the castle as his Cardiff residence. He turned Cathays Park into an enclosed parkland.

Following a critical public health report, the Cardiff Corporation established a new cemetery in Cathays. It was opened in 1859 and extended in 1887. E.T. Willows, a pioneer in aviation, and Jim Driscoll, the famous boxer whose funeral in 1925 attacted 100,000 mourners, are among those buried at Cathays. A poignant memorial was unveiled in the cemetery on the 50th anniversary of VE Day as a tribute to those who died in the Cardiff Blitz, many of them buried in a mass grave.

Apart from the cemetery, Cathays was almost entirely rural when it became a suburb of Cardiff in 1875. To the south lay the Bute Estate, while to the north were a number of scattered farms. There were just a few streets leading off Woodville Road and Cathays Terrace, but during the next 25 years the urbanisation of Cathays was virtually completed. Only Allensbank and Wedal farms were still under cultivation and by 1914 they also became no more than local placenames.

A crucial moment in the history of Cardiff occurred in 1898, when the 3rd Marquis of Bute sold 59 acres of land in Cathays Park to the council for the building of a new town hall.

The memorial to the victims of the Cardiff Blitz. Among the names are those of the Palmer family who lived in Wyverne Road. All 10 of them were killed when a landmine fell near their Anderson shelter in April 1941.

He imposed strict conditions regarding the development of the site. The avenues of trees were to be preserved, there were to be no commercial buildings and the area was to be exclusively retained for civic, cultural and educational purposes. The result of Bute's foresight was one of the finest civic centres in the world, the envy of every other city in Britain.

Cardiff became a city in 1905, just as the new council headquarters was being completed. The City Hall is an architectural gem, erected at a cost of only £129,000, and over the years other fine buildings were to make their bow. University College moved from Newport Road to Cathays Park in 1909 and the expanding needs of the university have led to further developments since that time. The attraction of this beautiful setting led to the establishment of the National Museum of Wales to 'teach the world about Wales and the Welsh people about their fatherland'. The Welsh National War Memorial was unveiled in 1928 and the scene around this cenotaph is deeply moving when crowds gather on Remembrance Sunday. The largest building in Cathays Park, though not the most elegant, is the Welsh Office. When local councils were invited to choose a capital for Wales in 1954, the choice was overwhelmingly in favour of Cardiff, almost certainly because its civic centre reflected so many aspects of Welsh life.

As a devout Catholic, the 3rd Marquis contributed generously towards the building of Nazareth House, which was opened in 1875 to provide acommodation for 65 orphan girls and 46 impoverished elderly people. The home was a popular

Cardiff's magnificent Civic Centre, looking towards Cathays in 1990. In the centre is the City Hall, behind which lie Queen Alexandra Gardens and the Welsh Office. The National Museum of Wales is on the right with the buildings of University College behind it. On the left are the Law Courts with the Police Headquarters to the rear.

Nazareth House, 2002. In front of this impressive Victorian Gothic building is the statue of Our Lady.

local charity and one of its most generous benefactors was Jim Driscoll. In a memorable act of unselfishness, he rejected the chance to fight for the Featherweight Championship of the World in New York because he had promised to return home for a charity event at Nazareth House.

When Maindy Barracks was opened in 1871, few could have foreseen the turbulent events of the 20th century in which the barracks would take part. Troops of the Welsh Regiment marched out from Maindy to fight the Boers in 1899 and in August 1914 the barracks was inundated with a flood of volunteers, responding to Kitchener's call to arms. Gladstone School was just one of several emergency recruiting stations hastily opened to deal with the rush.

A hero of World War One was Sergeant Major Frank Barter who lived at 60 Daniel Street. He won the Victoria Cross for his 'conspicuous bravery' at Festubert in 1915, when he attacked a German position with eight volunteers, capturing 100 prisoners and 500 yards of enemy trenches. He was given a hero's welcome on his return to Cathays and later in the war was awarded the Military Cross for further acts of courage.

In World War Two, American GIs were transferred to Maindy Barracks, pursued by prostitutes from Liverpool who comandeered an area near the former Maindy Pool. The footpath between Gelligaer Street and New Zealand Road soon became known as the 'BURMA Road' (Be Undressed and Ready My Angel). Local residents were appalled at scenes of debauchery in ramshackle huts or on open ground but

Maindy Barracks in the early 20th century. Until 1960 all recruits for the Welsh Regiment did their preliminary training at this centre.

protests to the Chief Constable proved futile. The Americans were responsible for the discipline of their troops and usually turned a blind eye to these escapades.

Maindy Pool was an old clay pit that had gradually filled with water and it claimed several lives before a petition to fill in the 'bottomless pit' was heeded. It took eight years of tipping to complete this process, during which one lorry sank and its driver was drowned. Plans to develop the site were delayed by World War Two but in 1948 the building of Maindy Stadium began. It was to stage events in baseball, athletics and boxing but it is best remembered for its role as a cycle track in the Empire Games of 1958. When the stadium was closed and replaced with a leisure complex, part of the site rather ironically became a swimming pool.

Most of the housing in Cathays is indistinguishable from similar suburbs in Cardiff but an exception is the elegant St Anne's Square at the northern end of Cathays Park. These splendid houses, set in private grounds, are among the most desirable in Cardiff. Despite the rapid urbanisation of Cathays, extensive parkland exists around the civic centre. The Gorsedd Gardens, Queen Alexandra Gardens, Bute Park and Blackweir offer an oasis from traffic in a busy city centre.

For many years Maindy Pool was an eyesore and a cause of many fatal accidents. After World War Two, the land was used to build Maindy Stadium.

Further Reading:

Chappell, E.L. *Cardiff's Civic Centre*, Priory Press, 1946.

Lee, B. *Cathays, Maindy, Gabalfa and Mynachdy*, Chalford Publishing Company, 1998.

CYNCOED AND LAKESIDE

Population: 10,490

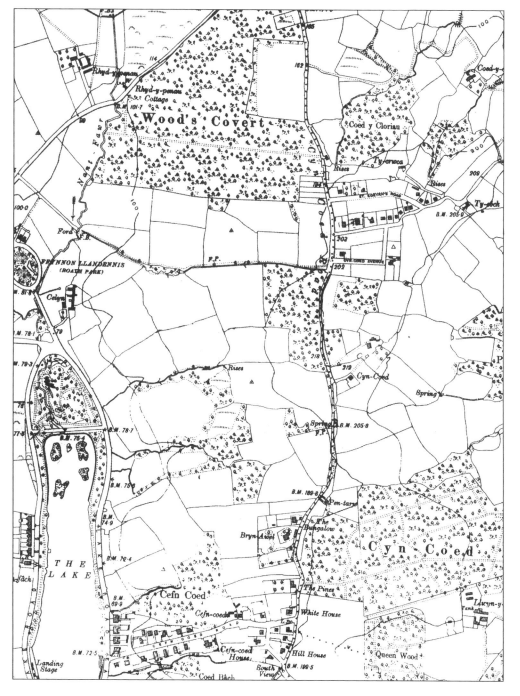

Roath Park Lake is instantly recognisable on this map of 1922 but Cyncoed Road is now much wider and the open countryside is covered with upmarket housing.

Roath Park Lake in 1896, two years after it was opened. A few councillors claimed that no one would visit the park because it was so far out of Cardiff. This point of view was soon to change.

A century ago Cyncoed Road was still an ancient trackway leading from Penylan to Lisvane. The road was bordered by farms, a few dwelling houses and extensive areas of woodland. From the wooded ridge, after which Cyncoed is named, streams such as the Nant Fawr Brook poured down the hill to create what one observer described as a 'malarial bog'. At that time few people would have foreseen that this unpromising landscape would become one of the most select suburbs of Cardiff.

The first step was taken in 1887, when the Cardiff Corporation was seeking a site for a new public park. The 3rd Marquis of Bute and other landowners offered 121 acres of despised marshland, free of charge, to provide a park with a lake, pleasure gardens and playing fields. The development of Roath Park cost £62,000, half of which was used to drain the land and create the lake. Amid great celebrations the new park was formally opened by the Marquis on 20 June 1894.

Soon trams were travelling to Roath Park from every part of Cardiff. Boating on the lake became a special attraction as it still is. The most prominent feature of the lake is the lighthouse, which was dedicated in 1915 to the memory of Captain Scott. Crowds cheered Scott's attempt to be the first man to reach the South Pole when his ship, the *Terra Nova*, set out from Cardiff in June 1910. Few among them could have imagined the cruel death that awaited Scott and his faithful band of comrades after the bitter experience of discovering that their Norwegian rival, Amundsen, had reached the Pole before them. There are further reminders of the Scott connection with Cardiff at the Discovery Inn on the Lakeside Estate and the Royal Hotel in the city centre.

The lighthouse on Roath Park Lake recalls the heroism of Captain Scott and his companions who sailed from Cardiff to the Antarctic in June 1910. A model of their ship, the Terra Nova, *can be seen on top of the lighthouse.*

Cefn Coed farmhouse had a remarkable escape in World War Two, when a bomb landed in the bedroom and came to rest against a wardrobe without exploding.

This view of Cyncoed Road in the 1930s, looking towards its junction with Rhydypenau Road, is very similar today.

Not surprisingly, the magnificent views overlooking Roath Park soon attracted property developers. Large villas in Lake Road East, many of them now transformed into luxury flats and nursing homes, were occupied by shipping magnates and coal exporters before 1914. There were also fine houses on Lake Road West and after World War One an array of streets sprang up on this side of the park, patriotically named after admirals such as Jellicoe, Beattie and Cunningham.

A number of dwellings were built in Cefn Coed Road before 1914 and standing among them is the original farm house. The building dates back to the early 18th century, though an extension was added in the Victorian era. It was after World War One that the landscape around Cyncoed Road began to change its character, when high-quality houses were built on former farmland. By 1939 a major residential area extended from Rhydypenau Road to Llandennis Avenue and Hollybush Road. The houses were all individual in style and, sited in an idyllic setting, attracted many of Cardiff's wealthiest families to Cyncoed.

It was still not difficult to escape into the countryside. The Cardiff Golf Club occupied a considerable stretch of land to the north of the suburb and Llanishen Reservoir was within easy walking distance for most people. The Cyncoed Lawn Tennis Club, which was used as an anti-aircraft battery in World War Two, stood on the site of modern Brynderwen Close. Among the acres bordered by Lake Road East, Cyncoed Road, Cefn Coed Road and Llandennis Avenue, people could still ramble through open fields.

In 1923, as the parish church of Llanedeyrn lay some distance away, All Saints

was dedicated as a mission church on Cyncoed Road. Fifteen years later the Methodists established their 'chapel in a garden' a little further along the road at Westminster Crescent. It was rebuilt and enlarged in 1965 and more recently a thriving community centre has become a focus, not only for the church, but for other organisations as well.

The Cardiff Golf Club, founded in 1922, possesses one of the most beautiful courses in South Wales.

A few bombs fell harmlesly on the golf course during World War Two but tragedy occurred when a Spitfire crashed near the 12th green, killing its pilot. In the tense days of 1940, poles were inserted in the fairways to prevent an airborne invasion and the Home Guard patrolled the course, using the clubhouse as their headquarters. Later in the war there was a US army base in Cyncoed and, during the build-up to D-Day, it was a familiar sight to see hundreds of Sherman tanks trundling along Cyncoed Road.

In the 1950s the rural nature of Cyncoed vanished, when the insatiable demand for new homes led to a fresh encroachment on the countryside. The biggest development was the Lakeside estate, centred around Celyn Avenue, but there was also a major building programme further north where Hackerford Farm and Black Oak Farm had previously stood. The new houses were built for private ownership in keeping with the pre-war character of the district. As the population increased, Lakeside Primary School was built in Ontario Way and Ty-Celyn, later Cardiff High School, was built on the site of Celyn Farm. The high reputation of these schools is one reason why many parents choose to live in Cyncoed.

The Cyncoed campus of UWIC. Many new facilities have been added in recent years but this view would have appeared very similar in 1961, when the site was the Cardiff College of Education. The round building on the left is the library.

The Cardiff College of Education opened in 1961 to meet the demand for more teachers and is now one of the sites used by UWIC. Various courses are taught at Cyncoed but its fame stems from the PE department, which over the years has been attended by many Welsh sporting heroes. Lynn Davies, who later lectured in the PE department, was a student when he won a gold medal in the long jump at the 1964 Olympic Games. Huw Morris, Steve Watkin and Greg Thomas were cricketers who studied at the college and went on to play for England. The Welsh goalkeeper, Dai Davies, represents the world of football, but the college is most renowned for its conveyor belt of Welsh rugby internationals. J.J. Williams, John Deveraux, John Bevan, Clive Griffiths and, most famous of all, Gareth Edwards were all students at Cyncoed.

Property values in this prosperous middle-class suburb are very high and houses, built in the 1920s for £1,000, may now command a value 500 times greater. Older residents might mourn the loss of their open countryside in the last 40 years but they are still fortunate enough to live in one of the most desirable districts of Cardiff.

Further Reading:
Morgan, D. *Llanedeyrn, the Story of Our Parish*, Dennis Morgan, 1973.

ELY

Population: 16,370

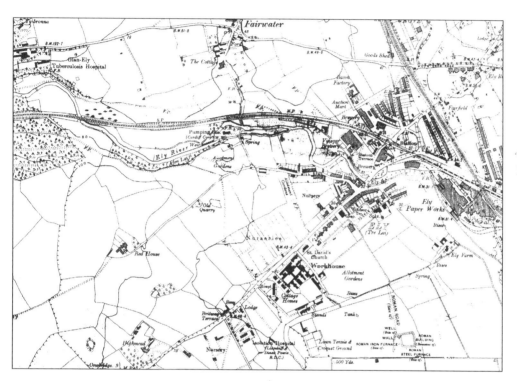

In this map of 1922, the little hamlet of Ely is clustered around the paper works and breweries. The northern side of Cowbridge Road was about to see a massive building programme which would engulf Red House Farm and the surrounding countryside.

There may have been a tiny settlement at Ely when the Romans built a road along the ancient trackway from Llandaff. After crossing the River Ely by a ford, the route continued along what is now Cowbridge Road West. In 1545 John Leland observed that the river was spanned by a stone bridge with two arches. Nearby was a small chapel, where travellers could pray and leave an offering for the maintenance of the bridge and the chapel.

After the Norman Conquest, the hamlet of Ely was granted to the manor of Llandaff, together with a fishery, a mill and later a tithe barn. The tithe barn was still in use in the 18th century, when Mill Road, little more than an alley at that time, led to the bishop's corn mill alongside the river at Cartwright Lane. The tiny population lived in cottages clustered around Ely Bridge and Mill Road. The highlight of their year was the annual fair on St Magdalen's Day, 22 July, which tended to be a rowdy affair, as copious draughts of ale were drunk while watching such pastimes as bull-baiting and cock-fighting.

Though in a dilapidated state, Ely Bridge assumed an importance before the Battle of St Fagans in May 1648 when Colonel Horton sent a detachment to defend it, thus preventing the Royalists from advancing on Cardiff. Roads generally were in

The Bridge Hotel, the shops and the houses have seen few changes since this photograph was taken in 1909. An exception is the old bridge with its four arches which was replaced two years later.

a deplorable state at that time and the Portway, as Cowbridge Road was known until the 19th century, was no exception. A complaint of 1697 records that the road at Ely was 'filled with water and was a danger to the King's subjects'. The Turnpike Trust set up in 1766 led to improvements and soon mail coaches were rattling through Ely on their way to Milford Haven. Ely Bridge was widened and strengthened in 1792 and remained in use until 1911, when the present bridge was constructed.

Ely provided Cardiff with its first supply of pure water following the cholera outbreak of 1849. The Cardiff Water Company bought the rights to the corn mill and built a pumping station to draw water from the river. It was carried by pipes to a reservoir at Penhill and from there it was distributed to the centre of Cardiff.

The opening of Ely Station in 1850 was described in the *Cardiff and Merthyr Guardian* as, 'not only a focal dispatch point for livestock but also a passenger station of no mean importance used by the inhabitants of Llandaff, Whitchurch, Fairwater, Radyr, Ely and all those villages and country houses bordering on the turnpike road for six miles westwards'. Though Ely was still regarded as 'a small village in the parish of Llandaff', the railway helped to bring new industries to the area, most of which congregated around the bridge.

Among these industries were two breweries. The Ely Brewery, established in 1855 to the north-east of the bridge, used water from its artesian well, thus prompting the

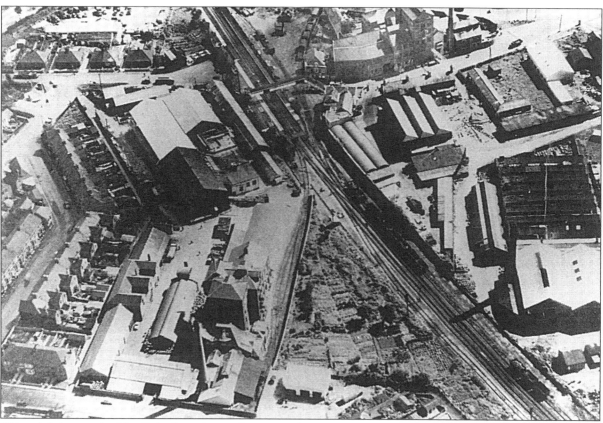

This aerial photograph of the 1950s shows Crosswell's Brewery (lower centre), separated by the railway line from Ely Brewery (top centre).

Ely Paper Mills, 1930. After more than 130 years of paper manufacturing, this site is now empty following its closure and demolition. How to make the best use of this large area is still under discussion.

A view of Grand Avenue in the 1930s. Running from Cowbridge Road to Green Farm Road, its width and grassy central reservation made it the most impressive thoroughfare on the Ely Estate.

slogan, 'Ely ales, the best in Wales'. Within 40 years, Crosswell's Brewery, which later became the Rhymney Brewery, was established on a site opposite its rival on the other side of the railway line. In 1959 the two companies merged and the older brewery was demolished. With an outlet of 750 pubs, the future appeared bright but in 1966 the new Ely Brewery fell prey to a takeover bid from Whitbread's. More than a century of manufacturing beer in Ely finally came to an end in April 1982 and, where two breweries once existed side by side, an industrial estate and houses now occupy the sites. Not far from the breweries, Samuel Chivers set up his factory in 1890. Famous for its vinegar, pickles and jam, Chivers' once employed 100 people but in 1977 the firm was sold to Fieldsman Preserves and closed a few years later.

The Ely Paper Works, which opened in 1865, was sited south-east of the bridge. Its most prosperous years began after Thomas Owen bought the works in 1877 and within 20 years it was the largest producer of newsprint in Britain. As late as 1990, when Arjo Wiggins Appleton became the owners, the future appeared bright as the company switched to the manufacturing of carbonless paper. Unfortunately, demand for this product fell in the age of the computer and 460 jobs were lost when the company ceased trading in 1999. Some of those made redundant were the fourth generation to work at the mill.

Until the end of World War One, these businesses made little difference to the growth of Ely, the population of which still numbered less than 1,000 in 1920. However, in his election address of 1918, Lloyd George promised 'homes fit for

heroes' and all post-war governments promoted a policy of slum clearance and better housing. In 1922 Ely became a suburb of Cardiff and, following the compulsory purchase of Red House Farm and Green Farm, nearly 3,500 council houses were built within two years. The entire estate north of Cowbridge Road was virtually completed before World War Two and won approval as an example of a garden suburb with 'its gabled cottages, low housing densities and the baroque patterns of the road layouts'. The houses were built to a high standard and electric lighting was installed in every property at a time when most homes were lit by gas. Many of these dwellings were built by the firm of Bright and Addicott, which began a small-scale business in Ely with a capital of £400. The quality of their work was so impressive that they were soon rewarded with major contracts. Houses at Ely were in great demand and first priority was given to families living in overcrowded conditions.

When the Western Cemetery was opened at Culverhouse Cross in 1936, a corner of it was made available to the Imperial War Graves Commission. Simple, white headstones serve as a reminder of servicemen who died in two world wars. At that time, despite the intensity of the building programme in Ely, the countryside was not far away. Caerau was still undeveloped south of Cowbridge Road and St Fagans, with its rural serenity, lay to the north.

However, since 1945 Ely has extended its urban growth, particularly in the

These 'gabled cottages' in Grand Avenue are an example of the thoughtfulness which went into town planning in Ely 80 years ago.

Despite the building of a southern bypass, Cowbridge Road West, seen here at its junction with Grand Avenue, remains among the busiest roads in Cardiff.

vicinity of Culverhouse Cross and Drope Road, where a major private housing estate has been built. The Copthorne Hotel, HTV Studios and a busy retail park have made further inroads to the green belt and have added to the traffic congestion at this western edge of Cardiff. The roundabout at Culverhouse Cross with its links to the M4, the Southern Bypass, Cowbridge and Barry, has become one of the busiest in Cardiff.

Further Reading:

Billingham, N. and S.K. Jones *Ely, Caerau and Michaelston-super-Ely*, Chalford Publishing Company, 1996.

Denning, R. *Long Lost Elysian Fields* in The Cardiff Book III, p.84–9, Stewart Williams, 1977.

FAIRWATER

Population: 13,680

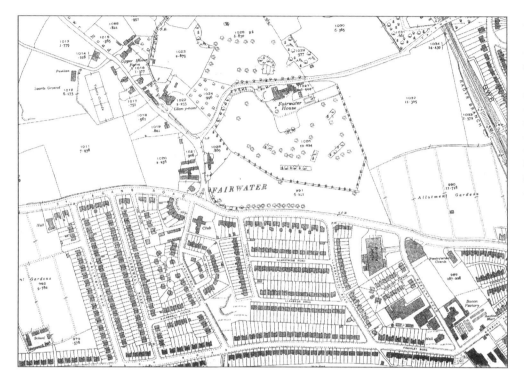

Fairwater in 1940. The area around the Green and south of St Fagans Road was developed by this time but large dwellings and Brook Farm still occupied open land to the north. This too would be filled with houses after World War Two.

Fairwater, or 'the Prebend of Fairwell' as early documents refer to it, was originally a possession of Llandaff Cathedral. In 1553 the lands were sold to Miles Mathew, before later passing first to the Romilly family and then in 1852 to William Sheward Cartwright, from whom Cartwright Lane takes its name. In the early 20th century just over 100 people lived in Fairwater and the district presented a picturesque rural scene. Howard Spring remembers happy boyhood days spent fishing in a stream, 'crossed by a railway bridge, whose embankment was at times like a long snowdrift, so thickly the dog daisies grew there'.

The heart of the district was to be found around Fairwater Green and the brook which trickled down Cartwright Lane on its way to the River Ely. On one side of the Green was Swiss Cottage, later known as the Smithy, a beautiful half-timbered house with mullioned windows and barley sugar chimneys. Near Swiss Cottage was the 18th-century Brook Farmhouse. On the opposite side of the Green stood a large chestnut tree, a semi-circle of conifers and a thatched cottage. Before World War Two, the conifers made way for the shopping centre and, when the cottage was destroyed in a fire, it was replaced by the Fairwater Hotel which became the home of the local Conservative Club in 1939.

The brook at Fairwater, c.1930. The thatched cottage across the road was destroyed in a fire and the Fairwater Hotel now stands on this site.

Ely Rise was once the home of W.G. David, whose initials can still be seen in the entrance porch. The property is now owned by the Fairwater Conservative Club.

Among the farming community of Fairwater there were several large houses. Fairwater Croft was the residence of Sir John Courtis, Lord Mayor of Cardiff. Ty-Gwyn in Fairwater Road was a substantial dwelling built for Harald Dahl and it was there in 1916 that his son, Roald, was born. Along the same road lay Fairwater House, which no longer exists as it was wrecked by vandals in 1994. Built in 1840 by David Vaughan, the property was owned in 1929 by Major Edgar David who, it was said, 'took great pride in the appearance of the village'. In 1949 it became one of Cardiff's first residential homes for the elderly.

The Davids were a very influential family in Fairwater. Possibly the most impressive residence in the district was the house designed by John Prichard in the mid-19th century for W.G. David at Ely Rise. The Gothic style of the house with its steep roofs and tall chimney stacks is still impressive. During World War Two the house was used by the Royal Observer Corps, 'the eyes and ears of the RAF', to plot the course of incoming enemy aircraft. After the war, the Fairwater Conservative Club purchased the property and turned it into one of the most thriving clubs in Wales.

Sometimes described as an Edwardian treasure, Ty Bronnau on the St Fagans Road was built by Charles Voysey and became the home of Hastings Watson. Legend has it that Ty Bronnau was haunted by a lady dressed in grey who was said to be the mistress of Mr Watson. More than one person claims to have been

The shopping centre at Fairwater Green. On the other side of the road is the Fairwater Hotel. The busy crossroads at this point contrasts with the peaceful calm of a hundred years ago.

Swiss Cottage, c.1914, with a hayrick in the garden. The barley sugar chimneys were shipped to America when the house was demolished in 1972.

awakened as the ghost tried to remove their wedding rings. When Ty Bronnau ceased to be a family home, it became part of the Glanely Tuberculosis Hospital. Founded after World War One, the hospital became a leader in the fight against this scourge and provided a school for nurses wishing to take the British TB Certificate. Later Ty Bronnau was used as the headquarters of the South Glamorgan Ambulance Service but, once the building was unoccupied, it was vandalised and eventually destroyed by fire in 1998.

Fairwater became a suburb of Cardiff in 1922 and by 1939 new houses covered the area between Wellwright Road and Ely Road. Since World War Two most of the countryside to the north and west of Fairwater has been urbanised. Brook farmhouse was bulldozed in 1957, as the farms around Plasmawr Road began to disappear. Now only the brook remains as a memory of bygone days. Waterhall Farm gave its name to one large development and, in the 1960s, agricultural land at Pentrebane provided space for another housing estate. Amid the shopping centres, schools, churches and other social amenities essential to a growing population, the suburb also provides Cardiff's only ski slope for those who wish to practise before trying the real thing.

Further Reading:
The Llandaff Society *Llandaff,* Chalfont Publishing Company, 1996.

GABALFA AND MYNACHDY

Population: 8,330

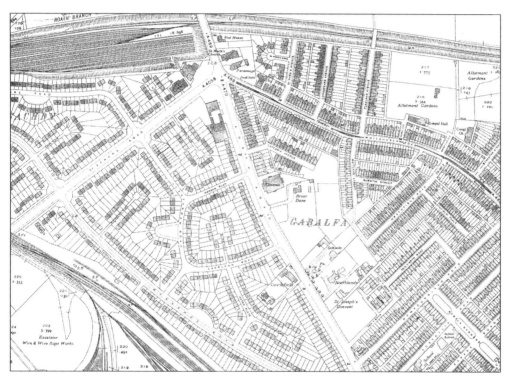

Gabalfa in 1942. St Athans Road has now become part of Western Avenue and the Gabalfa Flyover has been built at its junction with North Road and Whitchurch Road. The railway line and sidings to the north are no longer there.

For centuries Gabalfa was a sparsely populated hamlet in the parish of Llandaff. The name, meaning 'place of the ferry', is a reminder of how people crossed the river before a bridge was built at Western Avenue. An 1879 survey shows a few houses along North Road, among them Northlands, Heathlands and Maendy Lodge. The 18th-century farmhouse of Llystalybont lay close to Mynachdy Farm between North Road and the Taff Vale Railway. The manor of Llystalybont was once owned by Llantarnam Abbey, which may explain how Mynachdy, meaning 'a monastery', gained its name. The manor became a part of the Cardiff Castle Estate when the Earl of Pembroke acquired it following the Dissolution of the Monasteries. The farmhouse still exists and is now used by the council as a training and development centre.

St Mark's Church, built in a Decorated Gothic style, stood at the junction of North Road and Whitchurch Road. Previously, parishioners had met in a little schoolroom in North Road and the consecration of St Mark's in 1876 was a

Llystalybont farmhouse, c.1900. Farming ceased in 1918, as plans were laid to build the Mynachdy council estate. The thatched roof is gone but the farmhouse is still in use as a training centre for the council.

recognition that Gabalfa was about to become a parish in its own right. The population of the district was less than 500 at that time and its rural nature is indicated by a contemporary comment that the new church would be 'an adornment to the beautiful scenery amongst which it is placed'. The first vicar was John Davis, known as 'Sporting Jack' because of his love for hunting. He made a point of visiting his scattered parishioners on horseback in an attempt to preserve traditional rights of way.

By the outbreak of World War One, the open fields of Gabalfa were already disappearing and the land as far north as the modern interchange was brought into Cardiff's boundaries. The attractive terraced houses built in Whitchurch Road and around Africa Gardens, known originally as 'the colonies', were built in the first decade of the new century. In 1922 the entire parish became a part of Cardiff and the Mynachdy Estate, built on the former farm, was among the first council housing schemes in the city.

The Glamorganshire Canal, a prominent landmark in Gabalfa since 1794, passed through the Mynachdy Lock near the Excelsior Works of D. Morgan Rees. The company came to Cardiff in 1901 and became famous for its production of wire ropes. When manufacturing ceased in the 1990s, the site was incorporated into the Western Avenue Business and Retail Park.

The construction of Western Avenue from Ely Bridge to North Road followed a decision to build an inner bypass for Cardiff. It was finished in 1933 at a cost of £150,000 but the Ministry of Transport refused to finance a continuation of the route eastwards. The busy flow of traffic along North Road, Whitchurch Road and Western Avenue made its completion essential but 40 years were to pass before the

Mynachdy Lock before World War One. In the background are the chimneys of the Excelsior Wire Ropes Company.

Western Avenue leading towards St Mark's Church and vicarage, 1967. On the left is Gabalfa Library. All these buildings were about to disappear as Eastern Avenue took shape.

The Gabalfa Interchange, showing the slip roads off Eastern Avenue and the dual carriageway under the flyover, leading towards Western Avenue.

Queen offically opened Eastern Avenue in December 1971.

After World War Two, the Glamorganshire Canal was filled in and a large council estate was built alongside Western Avenue. Though this district was regarded as a part of Gabalfa, and both the primary school and the main avenue bear its name, the area is officially in the electoral division of Llandaff North.

The building of the Gabalfa Interchange had far reaching effects on the northern boundary of the suburb. Excavations were necessary to form the new highway linking Western and Eastern avenues. Two bridges were built above the avenue, as part of a roundabout controlling the traffic flow along five roads, while a flyover provided a third tier carrying vehicles directly towards the city centre. More than 100 houses as well as a number of other landmarks disappeared, among them the local library and the Regal Dance Hall. The most notable casualties of progress were St Mark's Church and its vicarage. A final service was held in April 1968, after which worshippers moved to their new church a short distance away in North Road.

The modern electoral district of Gabalfa scarcely compares with the original parish which included districts now in Llandaff North, Cathays, Llanishen and Whitchurch. Some years ago the population of Gabalfa, like many inner-city suburbs, was in decline, but that trend was halted when a huge campus at Llys-Tal-y-Bont, almost a village in its own right, was built to accommodate some of Cardiff's large student population.

Further Reading:

Gabalfa Parochial Church Council *A History of the Parish of Gabalfa*, St Mark's Parish Office, 1989.

Lee, B. *Cathays, Maindy, Gabalfa and Mynachdy*, Chalford Publishing Company, 1998.

GRANGETOWN

Population: 15,300

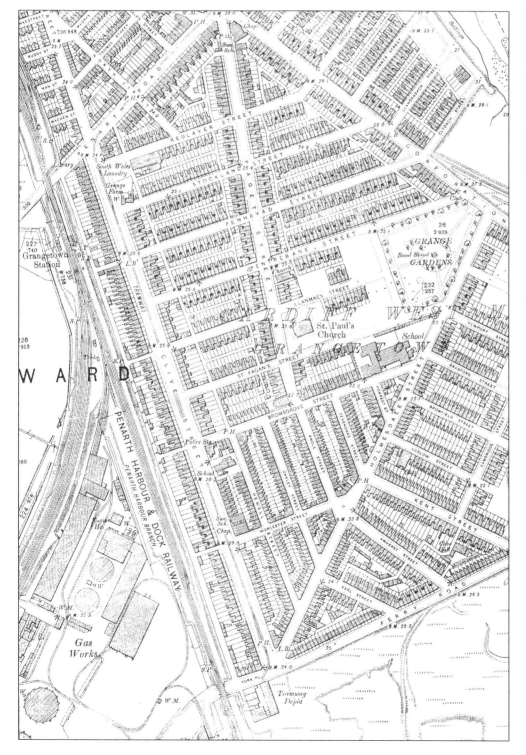

By 1901 Grangetown had assumed its modern appearance. In recent times, further changes have taken place in and around Ferry Road, where a retail park and new houses have been built at Windsor Quay.

Grangetown owes its name to the Moor Grange, a stretch of land between the Taff and Ely rivers. The Grange was granted to Margam Abbey by the Bishop of Llandaff in the early 13th century and was a rather bleak environment at that time. It has even been said that the Abbot sent disobedient monks to live and work there as a punishment. Remarkably, the Grange farmhouse, now more than 800 years old, still stands among Victorian houses in Clive Street. After the suppression of the monasteries, the Grange was sold to Edward Lewis of the Van. The property was leased to various tenants until it passed to the Plymouth Estate in 1730. Farming in the district continued into the early 20th century but by that time the surrounding area had dramatically changed.

In 1850 the isolation of the Grange ended when the Bute and Windsor estates shared the cost of constructing Penarth Road, together with its bridges across the Taff and Ely. Seven years later, plans were laid to build what Lady Windsor called 'the new town we may now expect to see spring up on the Grange'. Progress was slow at first but, when Grangetown became a suburb of Cardiff in 1875, the entire area was rapidly urbanised. In 1901 a local newspaper referred to Grangetown as 'a vast suburb of the Welsh Metropolis with a population of 17,000 souls'. Most of these people were working at the busy docks in Penarth and Cardiff.

Communications with Butetown were improved in 1890 when a Meccano-style bridge, named after the Duke of Clarence, provided a means of crossing the Taff. At that time the bridge was considered an engineering wonder and served the area until it was replaced with the present structure in 1976. The opening of the new Clarence

The Moor Grange was still a farm when this picture was taken in 1890 but it was not long before urban encroachment engulfed the historic farmhouse.

On 20 September 1890 the Duke of Clarence opened the Clarence Road Bridge. For nearly 90 years it remained the link between Grangetown and Butetown.

The premises of E. Turner and Sons in Havelock Place. The company did more than any other builder to change the face of Cardiff in the late 19th and early 20th century.

Sunday morning at the Marl in 1893. This crafty scheme to frustrate the closure of Welsh pubs on a Sunday was eventually thwarted by the opposition of the churches.

Road Bridge attracted national coverage on television as James Callaghan, in his capacity as MP for Cardiff South, cut the tape while making his first public appearance as Prime Minister.

In the late 19th and early 20th century, there were several thriving businesses in Grangetown. Some early enterprises such as an ironworks had failed but the Cardiff Gas and Coke Company concentrated its production near Ferry Road. Hancock's Brewery in Crawshay Street was famous throughout South Wales for many years, though S.A. Brain, once the great rivals of Hancock's, are now the owners of the brewery. In 1908 J.R. Freeman opened their cigar factory in North Clive Street before later moving to Penarth Road, where nearly 400 people are still employed.

Of all the businesses in Grangetown, none contributed more to the development of Cardiff than the building firm of Ephraim Turner in Havelock Place. When he came to Grangetown in 1885, Ephraim already had a fine reputation as a builder of bridges but in the 1890s his company constructed no fewer than 1,000 houses, 500 shops, 47 churches and 20 schools in the city. Turner also built some of Cardiff's most outstanding buildings. The extension of the Old Library and the former post office in Westgate Street were his creations but nothing surpasses his work in Cathays Park. The magnificent City Hall and the adjoining Law Courts were completed in 1905 at a total cost of £226,000.

St Paul's Church in Paget Street was a Turner building. The earliest Anglican church in Grangetown was the 'Iron Room', a temporary structure provided by Lady Windsor-Clive in 1879. It was erected with the minimum of cost, as the Baroness intended to provide a permanent building as soon as possible. Unfortunately, her sudden death led to a delay of 10 years before St Paul's was consecrated.

Grangetown was sited on a salt marsh and was always liable to be flooded from the sea. On 17 October 1883 everyone's worst fears were realised when a high tide burst through the dyke at Kent Street and flooded the streets to a depth of five feet. There was no loss of life but people hastily took refuge upstairs or, if they were trapped out of doors, awaited boats to rescue them.

Despite the intensity of building in Grangetown, space was found for recreation grounds. Grange Gardens, created from land donated by Lord Bute and Lord Windsor, is an attractive park and there is also a playing field at Sevenoaks Park in Sloper Road. The most famous recreational area in Grangetown is the Marl, built on the former marl pits. Close to the River Taff, it sports a bowling green and tennis courts but local people remember it for the prowess of its football and baseball teams, especially Grange Albion. Baseball has long been a popular sport in Cardiff and for years no team could match the Albion. One of their greatest triumphs came in World War Two, when the crew of an American warship challenged them to a game and were well beaten.

The Marl attracted the displeasure of the Temperance Movement in the 1880s, following the passing of the Welsh Sunday Closing Act. In an attempt to frustrate the act, up to 2,000 thirsty working men met at the 'Hotel de Marl' on Sunday morning. The drinks were free but customers were persuaded to make voluntary donations by two burly dockers. The churches, especially the Salvation Army, mounted a fierce campaign which eventually led to the termination of this ingenious experiment.

Grangetown suffered severely in the Blitz. Holmesdale Street, Ferry Road and the Saltmead district all had their casualties but the worst single incident occurred on 2 January 1941. The cellar of Hollyman's Bakery, at the junction of Stockland Street and Corporation Road, had been converted into an air-raid shelter and, when the siren wailed, 32 people trooped in. Soon afterwards the bakery was struck by a high-explosive bomb and all 32 were killed, including the Hollyman family.

In many respects Grangetown does not appear to have changed a great deal in the last hundred years. Few people now work in the docks and Penarth Road has gradually been filled with garages, warehouses and light industry. The principal changes in recent times have taken place around Ferry Road and Windsor Quay. Only 30 years ago Ferry Road was home to scrap-metal merchants, motor vehicle dismantlers, a sausage skin manufacturer and a licensed horse slaughterer. Since then

Some of the attractive dwellings at Windsor Quay which have transformed this part of Grangetown in recent years.

Windsor Quay has been redeveloped with attractive homes and a prosperous retail park. The area around Ferry Road is being landscaped and the prestige of the suburb will rise further if the much-heralded sports village is finally built.

Further Reading:

Jones, B. *Grangetown,* Chalford Publishing Company, 1996.

Clarke, I. *Grangetown, The Second Selection,* Chalford Publishimg Company, 1999.

HEATH

Population: 11,610

Until the 18th century the Heath was a large area of common land to the north of Cardiff. The Little Heath covered much of Cathays and Roath while Mynydd Bychan, the Great Heath, extended as far as Llanishen and Rhiwbina. Successive charters gave the burgesses of Cardiff the right to graze their animals or cut turf for fuel in this open countryside.

By the 17th century, as fewer people were exercising this privilege, undrained hollows became swamps, the number of trees proliferated and the Heath assumed a wild, desolate appearance. Despite efforts by the Cardiff Corporation to guard its traditional rights, smallholders, squatters and landowners began to fence off parcels of land for their own use. The extent of such intrusions is revealed by the complaint against Thomas Lewis of Llanishen in 1666, following his enclosure of 60 acres of land.

In the 1760s, part of the Great Heath became a racecourse with its starting point in the vicinity of 45–51 Heath Park Avenue. The circuit was two miles in length and

The northern part of Heath Park in 1961, flanked by King George V Drive with the King George V Memorial Gates at the centre. Most of these houses were built after World War Two. To the left, in the distance, are the ROF and other factories in Llanishen.

Heath Park Avenue. Two hundred years ago, the start and finish of the Heath Racecourse were situated near here.

the earliest races were usually individual contests. On 2 September 1765 Captain Mathew from Llandaff won £40 when his horse outpaced that of Lewis Morgan from Whitchurch. Within a few years the Corporation and the Marquis of Bute were contributing prize money for the Cardiff Races. When the Great Heath was enclosed in the early 19th century, the council retained the racecourse as a part of its allocation, even though racing at the Heath was beginning to lose its appeal. A newspaper report of 1825 comments: 'It is strange that in Glamorgan this noble sport should of late years have fallen off in the manner that it has done'. Formal meetings ended in 1849, when the course was sold to Wyndham Lewis for £3,100.

The Heath Enclosure Act of 1802 followed a request from the Cardiff Corporation to sell some of its common land to raise revenue. Half was awarded to the council while a sizeable amount went to freeholders who had a claim to rights of pasture. Most of them were rich, powerful families such as the Butes and the Lewises. The rest of the Great Heath was sold by auction and, in return for cancelling a number of fairly small debts, the Corporation transferred a proportion of its land to the Marquis of Bute at a bargain price. The Marquis was aided by John Wood, the Town Clerk, who also acquired a substantial estate for himself on the Little Heath. Some of these transactions seem to have been of a dubious nature and it was never clarified how the Corporation disposed of the money it received.

Squatters, who had fenced off small plots of the Heath for themselves, faced eviction and did not always leave quietly. John Bird, secretary to the Marquis, met

Heath House, built by the Lewis family, was a residence until 1938. Lying within Heath Park, it later became the venue for the Heath Citizens' Association until it was destroyed by fire.

The Heath Camp, 1942. The camp provided temporary accommodation for some of the troops rescued at Dunkirk. Later, British and American forces were based at the Heath and after the war the site was used as a teacher training college.

St Agnes Road after the raid of 18 May 1943. The landmine was among the last bombs to fall on Cardiff and amid this rubble nine people lost their lives.

resistance when he and the Deputy Sheriff tried to expel squatters in June 1799. He refers to fierce opposition from 'Amazonian women', armed with pitchforks and similar implements. Wisely Bird rode back to town to fetch the cavalry and after a fierce battle the squatters had to accept defeat, though for a long time afterwards Bird was taunted about his skirmish with the Amazonian women.

The landscape of the Heath was transformed following the Enclosure Act, as Heath Farm, Allensbank Farm and Ton-yr-Ywen Farm were created from the former rough pasture land. Much of the woodland was preserved and certain rights of way were upheld, among them the future Heathwood Road and Allensbank Road.

For more than a century, the district retained its rural aspect. The only buildings were a few cottages and Heathfield House, later known as 'Heath House'. This property was built by the Revd W. Price Lewis in 1840 and the Lewis family built up a considerable estate on the Heath through additional purchases. It was on their land that urbanisation began in the 1890s, mainly around Allensbank Road and Whitchurch Road. Other beneficiaries from enclosure, especially the Bute Estate, also leased their land for development and by the 1960s most of the Heath was an urban suburb.

Fortunately, in 1938 one area was preserved for recreational purposes when the Cardiff City Council purchased Heath House and its attractive parkland from Wyndham Clark, a descendant of the Lewis family. In 1949 the house became the headquarters of the Heath Citizens' Association and it survived until 1965, when it was destroyed by fire. Overlooked by the splendid King George V Drive, Heath Park remains one of Cardiff's finest recreational facilities, but it has served other purposes as well.

In World War Two, the War Office commandeered the park for military training and, later in the war, American forces were based there as part of the final preparations for D-Day. Before they were shipped to the docks, large numbers of vehicles were hidden under the trees from prying eyes.

Heath did not come through the war unscathed. On 18 May 1943, during the last air raid on Cardiff, a stick of bombs fell in Allensbank Road, severely damaging the Heath Hotel and a row of houses. An even worse incident occurred in St Agnes Road, when four dwelling houses were struck by a landmine. An eye witness remembered 'the huge column of black smoke rising like a leaping volcano with debris being hurled in all directions'. Seven people were killed outright by the bomb and two more died from their wounds.

After the war, some of the camp buildings on Heath Park provided accommodation for homeless families but in 1946 the site was designated as an emergency training college for teachers. Later, the Cardiff Training College offered two-year courses in PE as well as Arts and Crafts. The campus continued to serve a purpose, even after the Cardiff College of Education opened in Cyncoed, and it was not closed until 1974. Sixty years on, the wartime buildings are still used, two of

The University Hospital is the largest in Wales. As a teaching hospital, it not only gives training in medicine and dentistry but, as a completely integrated hospital and medical school, it also plays a vital role in research and has become the focus for medical care in south-east Wales.

The position of King George V Drive could hardly be better with its views across Heath Park, surely the most impressive 'front garden' in Cardiff.

them by the Heath Citizens' Association and the others by the city's leisure and sports department. The original parade ground serves as a car park.

Another part of Heath Park was swallowed up by the University of Wales Hospital. This teaching hospital and medical school was intended to benefit South Wales generally and one reason for choosing the Heath as its site was its proximity to Eastern Avenue and Northern Avenue, both under construction at that time. The Queen officially opened the hospital in December 1971 on the same day that traffic first began using Eastern Avenue.

Bordered by Eastern Avenue, Manor Way and the railway line from Cathays Cemetery to Caerphilly Road, the modern Heath has shrunk considerably from the great expanse of its mediaeval heritage. However, Heath Park provides a breath of fresh air which makes this suburb a very pleasant place in which to live.

Further Reading:

Williams, G. *Life on the Heath, the Making of a Cardiff Suburb,* Merton Priory Press, 2001.

LISVANE

Population: 3,540

Llysfaen, the Welsh name for Lisvane, translates into English as the 'stone court', suggesting that there was once a court house in the district which may have been used for collecting taxes. If this was the case, no trace of it remains and the earliest document relating to Lisvane is a charter of Bishop Nicholas in 1153, confirming that the tithes of St Denys's Church should be paid to Tewkesbury Abbey. A sizeable portion of land in Lisvane was also granted by the Norman conquerors to the abbey of Keynsham.

The Traveller's Rest at the summit of Thornhill, between Cardiff and Caerphilly, is over 350 years old and was once a coaching inn.

Near the Traveller's Rest at Thornhill, the gaunt ruins of Castell Morgraig are an impressive reminder of one man's rebellion against injustice. It is uncertain whether the partially completed castle was the work of the Normans or the Welsh, but this was where Llywelyn Bren made a defiant stand in 1316. The insurrection arose after the death of Gilbert de Clare at the Battle of Bannockburn. As he had no male heir, the lordship of Glamorgan passed temporarily to the King and the nobles he chose to administer the estate proved to be a disastrous choice. They imposed heavy taxes

The walls and earthworks at Castell Morgraig have become eroded by time but it was here that Llywelyn Bren made a courageous stand against overwhelming odds in 1316.

St Denys's Church from the south, 1981. The saddle-back tower was built at the time of the restoration in 1878 and is one of the church's most interesting features.

at a time of famine and great hardship, showed hostility to traditional Welsh customs and accused Llywelyn Bren, the much-respected bailiff previously appointed by de Clare, of creating unrest.

Unable to obtain satisfaction, Llywelyn raised his standard at Whitchurch in January 1316 and, with an army perhaps 10,000 strong, he wrought havoc with fire and sword throughout Glamorgan. From Neath to the Wye, castles, villages and mills were attacked and razed to the ground. The mill at Whitchurch was destroyed and even mighty Caerphilly Castle came under siege.

On 12 March 1316 a powerful royal army set out from Cardiff Castle to bring the rebels to heel and, though Llywelyn fought bravely at Castell Morgraig, the end was never in doubt. Greatly outnumbered, Llywelyn withdrew and retreated to Ystradfellte where he surrendered. For two years he languished in prison. The King was prepared to pardon him but Hugh Despenser, the new Lord of Glamorgan, persuaded him otherwise and Llywelyn was brought back to Cardiff Castle, where he was cruelly executed as a traitor. Justice was done some years later when his lands and privileges were returned to his sons. They became the forefathers of the Lewis family, who were to play an important part in the affairs of Llanishen and Lisvane.

After the Dissolution of the Monasteries, Edward Lewis of the Van purchased the Keynsham lands in Lisvane, while the Tewkesbury property was acquired by Sir Roger Kemys. The Lewises were generous benefactors and in 1728 a grant of £23 from Mary Lewis of New House was provided for the 'teaching and apprenticing of poor children in the parishes of Llanishen and Lisvane'. The charity is still active though now applied in a wider context. Another legacy from Mary provided money for the relief of the poor which is still distributed just before Christmas.

For centuries the rich, fertile soil of Lisvane yielded a bountiful harvest of grain which was processed in the local mills. There were several large, prosperous farms but at the heart of the tiny hamlet, which in 1841 had a population of 207, there was only a blacksmith, the Black Griffin Inn and half a dozen cottages grouped around the church. A shed at the rear of the church served as a small school but when the teacher, George Matthews, died in 1845 the school was closed. After 1867 Lisvane children attended the church school at Llanishen and a new primary school was not opened in the village until the early 20th century. Following its closure in the 1960s, it is now a community centre and the site of the local library.

Close ties have always existed between the churches of Lisvane and Llanishen and until recently they shared the same vicar or curate. One of the more eccentric characters was Benjamin Jones, who became vicar in 1814 and was known as the 'Old Parson'. He was a keen sportsman, fond of his gin and tobacco, but he showed little interest in St Denys's Church which was decaying into a roofless ruin with birds and animals sheltering in its walls. On wet Sundays Benjamin would pull the bell for matins and if only two or three turned up for the service, he suggested they ought to

A winter's day at Cefn Onn Park in 2002. When the rhododendrons and azaleas flower in May, the park becomes one of Cardiff's loveliest attractions.

adjourn to the Griffin Inn as it was not worth continuing. Eventually, repairs and restoration of the church were carried out at a cost of £500 in 1878, but little remains of its Norman origins apart from the walls of the tower and the south doorway with its holy water stoup.

In 1869, to meet the increasing demand for water in Cardiff, 19 acres of land in Lisvane was used to build a reservoir. It drew its water from local streams and was owned by a private company but in 1878 it was purchased by the Cardiff Corporation for £300,000. The reservoir did nothing to spoil the charm of the district and the council again showed vision in 1944, when it purchased the 200-acre Cefn Onn Estate from Edwin Prosser. Lying to the east of Llanishen Golf Club, it was turned into one of Cardiff's most beautiful parks.

Between the two world wars, only 50 new properties were built in Lisvane and the map of 1940 shows how the village had kept its rural atmosphere. The houses that were built, mainly along Ty-Llwyd road, now Lisvane Road, were luxurious and set in spacious grounds. Major building programmes did not intrude on the countryside until the 1950s. The land around the church was the first to be utilised, followed by the development of the Cherry Orchard Estate. With the emphasis always on private housing, property values in this prosperous district are among the highest in Cardiff. Lisvane became a suburb of the city in 1974 and in the next 20 years its population was to double. Despite the intrusion of the M4 motorway, the district has so far retained the atmosphere of a village community. Unfortunately, a scheme to build 4,000 houses from Pontprennau to Lisvane poses a threat to this peaceful tranquillity.

Further Reading:

Dowse, L. *Llanishen and Lisvane*, Koda Press, 1972.

Horton, G. *Llanishen from Village to Suburb*, Llanishen Local History Society, 1999.

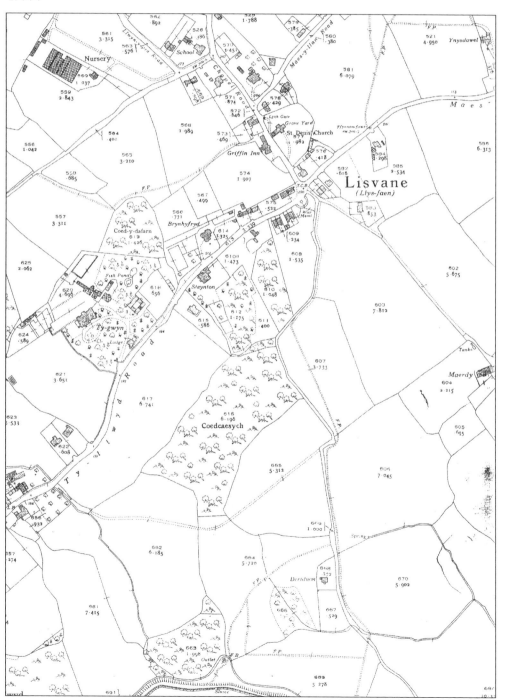

The village of Lisvane in 1940. At its heart is St Denys's Church, the Griffin Inn, the school and a few large dwellings. Now the fields to the left of Ty Llwyd Road (Lisvane Road) are covered with houses built after World War Two.

LLANDAFF

Population: 9,040

The Green at Llandaff before World War One. The cross, where Archbishop Baldwin and Giraldus Cambrensis preached the Third Crusade, was restored in 1897 and only the lower part of it now remains.

Llandaff Cathedral is a site of great antiquity established, so *The Book of Llandaff* tells us, by St Teilo on the banks of the Taff which gives Llandaff its name. The monastery became a focus of Christianity in the Welsh kingdom of Morgannwg but, after the Norman Conquest, Bishop Urban began the task of rebuilding the cathedral in stone. Progress was slow owing to a lack of funds and so the cathedral combines a variety of architectural styles. Norman and Gothic features are clearly visible, while the 15th-century Jasper Tower was built in the Perpendicular style.

In 1188 Archbishop Baldwin, accompanied by the Welsh bishop and chronicler, Giraldus Cambrensis, stood at the cross on the Green to recruit volunteers for the Third Crusade. Despite the animosity between the Welsh and their Anglo-Norman conquerors, they put aside their differences and, as Gerald observed: 'The business of the cross being publicly proclaimed at Llandaff, the English standing on one side and the Welsh on the other, many persons of each nation took the cross'.

Both the bishop and the archdeacon had their own castles at Llandaff. The Bishop's Castle, erected in the 13th century near the Green, was likened by a later

writer to 'the stronghold of any Norman robber, the lair of the wolf of the fold, rather than the dwelling of its shepherd'. The Archdeacon's Castle, where Henry II was once entertained, was also impressive. When Owain Glyndwr rampaged through Glamorgan in 1404, he had little sympathy for the hierarchy of the Church and, according to Adam of Usk, he scourged Llandaff 'like a second Assyrian, the rod of God's anger'. Owain left the Bishop's Castle and the Bell Tower as picturesque ruins but he obliterated the Archdeacon's Castle completely. The cathedral was spared but 20 years later the bishop was still complaining that the building, its books and its ornaments were in a pitiful state after Owain's onslaught.

Llandaff Cathedral was never as wealthy as its English counterparts. Even before the Reformation, the bishops were forced to sell church assets to meet everyday needs. The principal beneficiaries were the powerful Mathew family, who were among the leading landowners of Glamorgan in the 15th century. The different branches of the family exercised a powerful influence over Llandaff, Pentyrch and Radyr. A number of them rest in splendid tombs at Llandaff Cathedral, one of the most impressive being that of Sir David Mathew, standard bearer to Edward IV at the Battle of Towton. He obtained the lease to the manor of Llandaff and in 1553 his great-grandson, Miles Mathew, purchased the estate outright, including the manor house of Bryn-y-Gynnen.

This short-sighted policy of selling and leasing lands at bargain prices did nothing to improve the condition of the cathedral and in 1603 Bishop Godwin gloomily predicted that it would, 'in a short time fall to the ground without some extraordinary relief'. Matters were not helped by the absence of bishops who spent most of their time at their palace in Mathern near Chepstow.

The Civil War added to the cathedral's problems. On Easter Sunday 1646, Parliament's troops burst into the church and, after drinking the communion wine, marched the clergy and congregation to the gaol at Cardiff. There they were forced to listen to a Puritan sermon for three hours, while their books and other treasures were burnt before their eyes. The cathedral itself was turned into a stable, an ale house and a post office. The choir became a calf pen and the font a pig trough.

Years of abuse inevitably took their toll. In 1696 the great bell toppled from its moorings and seven years later the battlements of the Jasper Tower were damaged in a storm. In 1723 an even worse storm led to the collapse of the South-west Tower and the destruction of 50 feet of the nave. With limited funds, John Wood, the famous architect of Bath, built an Italianate temple within the ruins which B.H. Malkin described in 1803 as 'an outrageously, incongruous appendage of modern finery'.

Throughout these centuries, in keeping with the poverty of its church, the village of Llandaff had few attractions for its visitors. There were some elegant residences but Malkin expressed 'considerable surprise and disappointment', as he contrasted the mean streets and humble cottages of Llandaff with the finer, cleaner cathedral cities of England. John Speed's map of 1610 shows a village of about 60 houses with

A portrayal by Browne Willis of the 17th-century cathedral from the south. In the foreground is the South-west Tower. When it collapsed on the nave in 1723, the cathedral was exposed to the elements for more than 100 years.

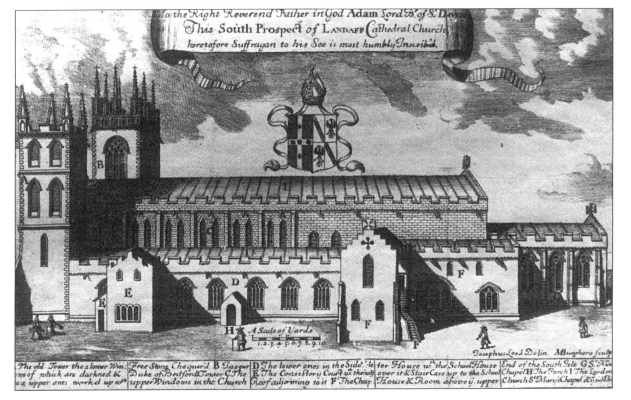

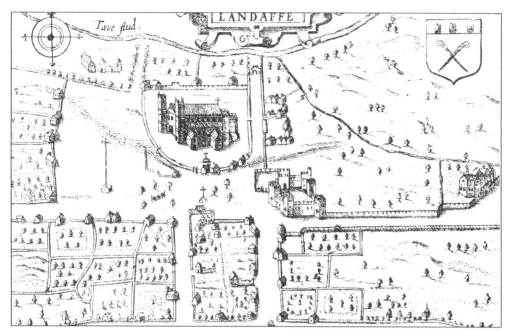

John Speed's map of Llandaff, 1610. High Street (right) and Heol Fair are the roads leading to the castle and cathedral. The lane from the Bishop's Castle to Bryn-y-Gynnen no longer exists.

plenty of open spaces. The cross, the maypole and the stocks can all be seen on the Green. From the castle a lane leads to the rambling, gabled manor house of Bryn-y-Gynnen. In the 18th century it was rebuilt for Admiral Thomas Mathew and renamed Llandaff Court. The Admiral chose not to live there after commenting that

he had spent enough years on a three-decker ship and had no wish to die in one. Llandaff Court served as the Bishop's Palace from 1850 until 1958.

The right to hold a Whitsun Fair on the Green was granted to the bishop by King John in 1205. The fair was an important source of income but by the 19th century it had become a rowdy occasion. In 1880 it was decided to discontinue this annual event and a few years later the Green was enclosed.

The task of restoring the cathedral after its long years of neglect was entrusted to John Prichard, the diocesan architect, whose father was the vicar of Llandaff. He demolished Wood's Italian temple and reconstructed

Llandaff Cathedral after its Victorian restoration, showing Prichard's Tower on the right, together with the Jasper Tower and the mediaeval West Front.

When the Cathedral School was revived in 1880, this pleasant, ivy-clad building on the Green was its first home.

In 1958 the school moved to Llandaff Court, which was built in 1744–51. It had originally been built for Admiral Thomas Mathew but in 1850 became the Bishop's Palace.

Young ladies relax in the grounds of Howell's School in 1880. In its early days the school offered 30 places to 'orphan inmates' and 30 places to 'pay boarders', but by 1900 there were also 75 day pupils.

High Street, Llandaff, c.1909. On the left-hand side of the road is the old Church in Wales School and the Butcher's Arms. On the right, in the distance, is the Bishop's Castle.

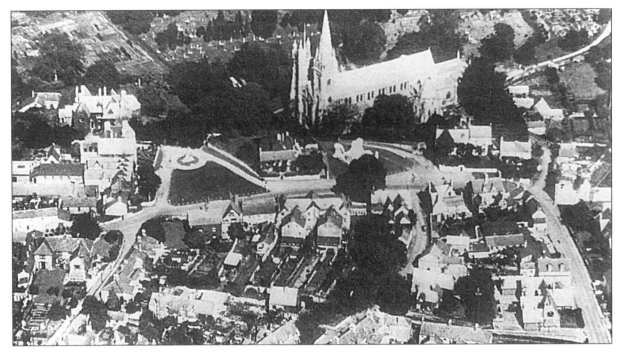

The village of Llandaff has seen few changes since this aerial photograph was taken in 1936. High Street on the right leads up to the Green and the cathedral. The allotments in the top left corner are now a wildlife site.

the presbytery and nave in a sympathetic manner to blend with its mediaeval characteristics. The tower that had collapsed in 1723 was replaced with a graceful spire that bears Prichard's name. One interesting feature was the row of sovereigns' heads, beginning with William I on the south wall and continuing along the north wall. Prichard's partner was J.P. Seddon, who commissioned a number of fine art works from the Pre-Raphaelite School, the most splendid of which is Rossetti's *Seed of David*. On 13 July 1869 a great thanksgiving service was held to celebrate the restoration of the cathedral.

Prichard's contribution to the architecture of Llandaff was not restricted to the cathedral. Other examples of his work in the village include the Probate Registry and St Michael's College in Cardiff Road. Many of the buildings on the Green were designed by him and the result is one of the most agreeable views in Cardiff.

The Cathedral School occupied premises on the Green when it was reopened by Dean Vaughan in 1880. An earlier school had been abandoned in the 17th century because of the cathedral's poverty but the new premises offered an education to 'the sons of gentlemen', with choral scholarships offered to boys chosen for the cathedral choir. In 1958 the school moved to the former Bishop's Palace at Llandaff Court and it is now the only surviving choir school in Wales.

Roald Dahl was a pupil at the Cathedral School between 1923 and 1925. In his autobiography, *Boy*, he recalls how he and his friends put a dead mouse in a sweet jar at the detestable Mrs Pratchett's shop, which may have been next to Spencer's Row in Bridge Street. Inevitably painful retribution followed and Roald's mother was so shocked by the beating he received that she took him from the school and sent him as a boarder to St Peter's in Weston.

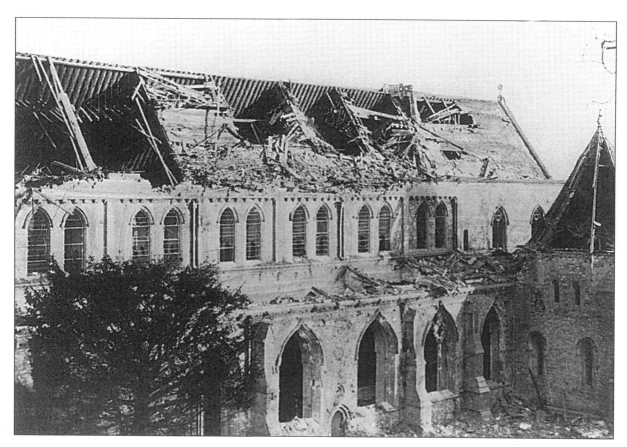

Howell's School for Girls in Cardiff Road is named after Thomas Howell, a 16th-century merchant of the Drapers' Company in London. His charity to provide dowries for orphan girls became redundant 300 years later, when a Parliamentary commission decided that the money should be used to provide schools for girls in Llandaff and Denbigh. Howell's has won a great reputation since it opened in 1859 and among its famous pupils is Charlotte Church who, at the age of 17, is an international celebrity possessing, so it has been said, 'the voice of an angel'.

By the early 20th century, Cardiff Road and Palace Road were splendid thoroughfares within walking distance of the cathedral. Even more exuberant were the splendid mansions of Cardiff's wealthier citizens. James Insole was a coal owner who used some of his fortune to build Insole Court, now owned by the city council. Sir Edward Stock-Hill, whose father had constructed one of the earliest dry docks in Cardiff, built Rookwood House, which was renowned for its magnificent gardens and is now used as a hospital.

Following its incorporation into Cardiff in 1922, it was inevitable that Llandaff lost some of its rural charm. Houses were built in and around Western Avenue and, as this new highway was constructed, the ancient Llandaff mill was demolished. The road also cut into the stretch of open countryside which had hitherto extended from the centre of Cardiff to the cathedral.

The chequered history of Llandaff Cathedral continued in World War Two, when

The nave of Llandaff Cathedral after the Blitz. Only Coventry among British cathedrals suffered greater damage during the war.

it was struck by a landmine on 2 January 1941. Ancient graves and tombstones were hurled like missiles more than half a mile away. The summit of the Prichard Tower was dislodged and its truncated appearance became a notable landmark for years afterwards. The roof of the nave collapsed and the beautiful Great West Window was shattered, but fortunately the Rossetti Tryptych and 12 priceless stained-glass windows had been safely stored.

Not until 1960 was the cathedral restored to its former glory. Generally, the restoration was based on Prichard's design, but the opportunity was taken to build a processional way and a memorial chapel dedicated to the Welsh Regiment. The nave was given a more open appearance, though Epstein's statue of Christ in Majesty caused some controversy.

Inevitably Llandaff has changed since World War Two. BBC Wales has moved into new studios in Llantrisant Road and a large housing estate has been built at Danescourt. New educational establishments include the Bishop of Llandaff High School and the Llandaff Technical College, now amalgamated with other colleges to form UWIC. Amid these changes, the heritage of the past has been better protected in Llandaff than in many suburbs of Cardiff. The narrow streets of Heol Pavin and Heol Fair, together with the ruins of the Bishop's Castle and the Bell Tower, evoke memories of a bygone age. Above all, the essential spirit of Llandaff is reflected, as it has been for so many centuries, through its ancient, indestructible cathedral.

Further Reading:
Hilling, J.B. *Llandaff Past and Present*, J.B. Hilling, 1978.
Llandaff Society *Llandaff*, Chalfont Publishing Company, 1996.
Morgan, D. *The Cardiff Story*, Dennis Morgan, 2001.
Thomas, E.S. *Llandaff Cathedral, A Pictorial History*, Pitkin Pictorials, 1970.

LLANDAFF NORTH

Population: 8,250

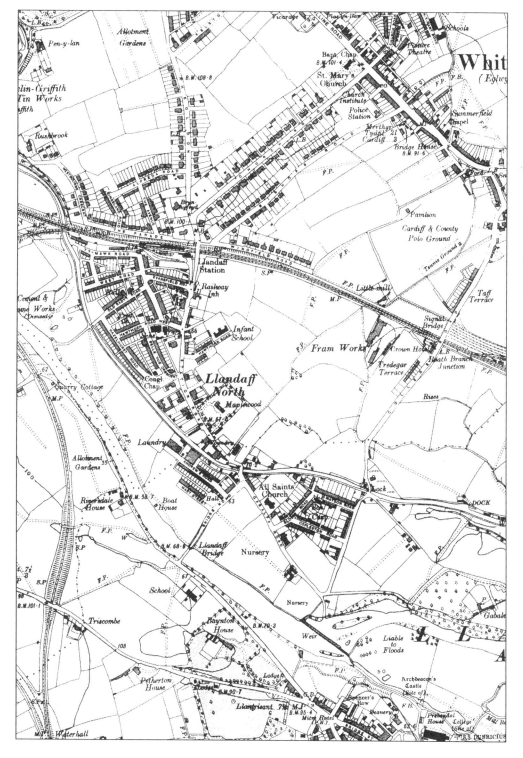

In this map of
1922, Llandaff
North lies between
the River Taff to
the south and the
railway line to the
north. The
Glamorganshire
Canal flows
through the suburb
from Whitchurch
towards Gabalfa.
Nowadays, the
electoral district of
Llandaff North
extends as far as
Western Avenue
and includes much
of the Gabalfa
housing estate.

The Eagle Foundry at Llandaff Yard, 1890. The site in Station Road is now occupied by the garage of James and Jenkins.

Llandaff North lies across the river from Llandaff and has been a suburb of Cardiff since 1922. The district was already a busy place before the end of the 19th century and there were enough children living in the area to warrant the building of Hawthorn School. By 1920 the neat, terraced houses of the streets near Llandaff Bridge and around Station Road were virtually completed. Both the Methodists and the Anglicans had their own churches and All Saints was described as 'a chapel of ease to the cathedral'. The church was badly damaged in World War Two and, in common with the cathedral, it rose like a phoenix from the ashes.

For a long time, Llandaff North owed much of its importance to the Glamorganshire Canal. When Merthyr was the 'iron capital of the world', the canal was its principal highway to the port of Cardiff. Rather like railway sidings, a wharf or yard was needed at every township along the canal to assemble, load and unload cargo. Hence the district was known as Llandaff Yard until 1910. The building of the railways lessened the canal's importance but it continued to act as a distribution point for industries lying along its banks. Some of these were not for the squeamish. The South Wales Manure Company steamed bones from slaughtered horses into manure, while another firm manufactured fiddle strings and similar articles from animal gut. There were also a number of patent fuel works, a soap factory and the Crown Matchworks.

Evans' Eagle Foundry was sited adjacent to Llandaff Lock, where barges deposited their raw material from the iron works of Merthyr. The foundry was not large but remained in business until the 1930s. Street signs, manhole covers and drain covers, inscribed with the firm's insignia, 'Evans, Llandaff', can still be seen in Cardiff today.

That area of Llandaff North between the canal and the railway line remained largely rural until after World War Two. Apart from a few houses and the Crown Hotel, College Road was just a country road linking Llandaff North with Whitchurch. The only exception was the Gwaun-tre-Oda Engineering Works, near the railway line, which was later taken over by the Fram Construction Company.

A bridge across the Taff has marked the approach to Llandaff North from Llandaff for hundreds of years. In May 1648 Colonel Horton and his army crossed the river at this point as they hastened to the Battle of St Fagans. The modern visitor has a choice of pleasing views while crossing the bridge. On one side are the playing fields of Hailey Park and on the other is a picturesque view of the cathedral.

The old industries that thrived along the banks of the Glamorganshire Canal are no more and the open countryside, which once led to Western Avenue, Gabalfa and Whitchurch, has been swallowed up by modern housing development. The canal was filled in after World War Two and now only a green sward near the Cow and Snuffers marks its route.

This pub, originally known as the Red Cow, is the oldest hostelry in Llandaff North, though much of it was rebuilt in 1905. It seems to have gained its unusual name from the lyric of a song in a musical farce, first performed in Dublin. A bust of Benjamin Disraeli can be seen at the first floor level. His secretary maintained that the great man, intrigued by the name, once spent a night there. Disraeli denied this story but he was a friend of Wyndham Lewis who owned much of Llandaff North. When Lewis died, Disraeli married his widow. Her name was Mary Anne and,

The bridge crossing the river to Llandaff North has been replaced and widened since this scene of 1925. Hailey Park, on the left, was presented to the city the previous year.

The lock of the Glamorganshire Canal at Llandaff Yard, 1910. The Cow and Snuffers public house has associations with Disraeli and beyond lie cottages which were probably built for industrial workers employed near the canal.

though she was much older than he was, the marriage proved to be a real love match. More than once, she mischievously boasted, 'Dizzy married me for my money but if he had the chance again, he would marry me for love'.

Further Reading:

Llandaff Society *Llandaff,* Chalfont Publishing, 1996.

LLANEDEYRN AND PENTWYN

Population: 17,570

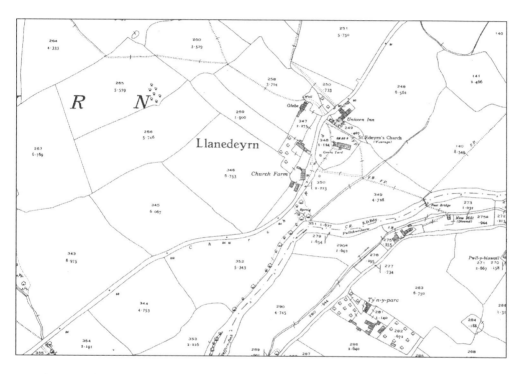

Llanedeyrn village in 1901 was part of a scattered rural parish, very different from the massive housing and industrial developments of recent times.

St Edeyrn, who gave the parish of Llanedeyrn its name, is a rather obscure figure, like so many of the Celtic saints. He travelled widely and there are churches dedicated to him in Brittany and North Wales. According to local tradition, Edeyrn was a fifth-century British prince who followed the Roman road from Caerleon to Cardiff. Finally, he arrived at the River Rhymney, where he built a wooden church.

The Normans rebuilt the church and, despite the restoration carried out in 1888, indications of their work remain in the windows and stonework of the nave. Originally the tithes of Llanedeyrn were paid to Tewkesbury Abbey, but their annals record that in 1236 they transferred their rights to Llandaff Cathedral. The same document also mentions the chapel of Llanforda which fell into disuse by the 16th century. It was converted into a cottage known as Ty'r Capel, the Chapel House, which stood in Coed-y-Gores near Chapel Wood as recently as 1950.

The vicarage at Llanedeyrn was the Glebe, a charming little cottage opposite the church. It was thatched until the 1970s and its interior, with sturdy beams and an

St Edeyrn's Church, 1973, showing its natural stone which has been painted white since that time. The 15th-century tower was built at about the time that Owain Glyndwr was rampaging through Wales and may have been intended as a watch tower.

The Glebe cottage, still thatched in 1973. As the vicar of Llanedeyrn also served the community of St Mellons and more recently All Saints in Cyncoed, the Glebe was frequently leased to secular tenants.

original wall of straw and wattle, dates back to the 15th century. For centuries, the parishes of Llanedeyrn and St Mellons had close ties and in 1558 David Lewis was vicar of Llanedeyrn, though his residence was at St Mellons.

The Anglican vicar, John Williams, was ejected from his living by Commonwealth commissioners in 1650 and no doubt the Puritan incumbent who replaced him suffered a similar fate when the monarchy was restored. At this time of religious persecution, the Quakers were particularly harshly treated but the sect had firm support in Llanedeyrn. There were 40 of them who met every Sabbath day in 1669 under the leadership of Thomas Quarrell and John Powell. Not until the Toleration Act of 1689 did religious persecution come to an end. As late as 1734 the vicar of Llanedeyrn showed that old animosities were not dead, when he grudgingly recorded the burial of William Rogers, 'a notorious dissenter'.

Jacobites in the district were prepared to support the cause of Bonnie Prince Charlie in 1745. David Jones, a labourer from Llanedeyrn, was presented at Cardiff Assizes, charged with uttering the treasonable words, 'God save King James ... with intent to seduce the liege subjects of the King'. David Morgan of Coed-y-Gores fared even worse after the Battle of Culloden, as he was one of the Prince's counsellors and, after being tried for treason, was beheaded on Kennington Common.

The Unicorn is over 300 years old and, for much of that time, it was a farmhouse as well as a taproom. Before the pub was sold to Ansell's in 1966, the Davies family had kept it for many years, brewing their own ale on the premises.

This little school at Penygroes, which has since been demolished, was opened in 1879 and served Llanedeyrn for nearly 90 years. In the church is a memorial to Lillie Addie, the much-loved first headmistress of the school.

Until the 20th century, Llanedeyrn was a typical rural community. Its farmers were tenants of the Kemys-Tynte family of Cefn Mably and farms such as St Julian's, Pentwyn, Tyn-y-Berllan, Malthouse and Llanedeyrn itself were the basis of the district's economy. The 1851 census shows that half the people living in Llanedeyrn were farm workers, though the village also boasted a blacksmith, a cobbler and a thatcher. The social centre of the hamlet was the Unicorn Inn, which in 1896 was described in these terms: 'A comfortable old thatched house, with an inn-kitchen of the picturesque sort, open chimney, oak settles, and fitches of bacon under the beams; and a native Welsh-speaking landlady'. The Unicorn has lost its thatched roof and some of its rustic charm, but it is still an attractive country pub.

In 1874 Charles Kemys-Tynte granted a quarter of an acre of land at Penygroes to provide 'a school for the education of children and adults… The premises may, if it is thought desirable, be used for penny reading and other such purposes which will help in the instruction of the parishioners'. Five years later, the school was opened to accommodate 60 children, though it was frequently closed in bad weather as children from the outlying farms had to tramp miles to get there. However, visitors to the school were glowing in their praise and a Diocesan Report of 1903 records that: 'The children in this little school have been very fully and carefully taught and passed as usual in all respects a highly satisfactory and creditable examination'. The school was a reflection of a small but closely knit community. The premises were

used for social events such as whist drives and dances and in 1919 there was a great celebration when the Llanedeyrn soldiers came home. Not surprisingly, there was great sadness among local people when the school closed in 1964.

Llanedeyrn, in common with other communities, lost many of its young men in World War One. A tablet in the church remembers Rowland Thomas of Tyn-y-Berllan Farm, who was killed in the battle for Jerusalem in 1917. In all, 10 young men from Llanedeyrn made the ultimate sacrifice and five more names were added to the Roll of Honour in World War Two.

In the 20th century the whole character of Llanedeyrn changed. The Kemys-Tynte Estate was broken up in 1921 and tenants were given the option to buy their farms. Part of Llanedeyrn came under Cardiff's jurisdiction as early as 1889, but most of it remained outside the city's limits until it was formally absorbed after the boundary changes of 1967.

It was then that Llanedeyrn and Pentwyn were transformed as the need for new housing led to rapid urbanisation. In 1961 the population of Llanedeyrn was only 1,377 but a huge housing development was to sprawl across an area where there were once just a number of scattered farms. Several new schools were built and Llanedeyrn High School has already in its short existence produced pupils of distinction, among them Colin Jackson, a great athlete respected and admired throughout the world. His sister Suzanne has also gained a reputation in the world of television and has appeared in several productions.

This view across the Pentwyn housing estate in 2002 makes it difficult to realise that this was agricultural land 30 years ago.

Set amid the light industry of Llanedeyrn and Pentwyn, the BUPA Hospital is a major employer and the largest private hospital in South Wales.

In its early days, people complained about the lack of facilities on the new estate but in 1974 the Maelfa Shopping Centre opened, and subsequently a health centre, a nursing home for the elderly, a library and a leisure centre have been established in the area. The construction of Eastern Avenue with its links to the M4 has led to an expansion of commercial activity, especially near its junction at Pentwyn, where the Posthouse, Campanile and Moat House hotels are convenient for business people. These hotels, light industry and the BUPA Hospital have brought much needed employment to the district. Only placenames such as Pentwyn, Chapelwood, Coed-y-Gores, Pennsylvania and Springwood now remind us of Llanedeyrn's rural past.

Further reading:
Morgan, D. *Llanedeyrn: The Story of Our Parish*, Dennis Morgan, 1973.

LLANISHEN

Population: 15,550

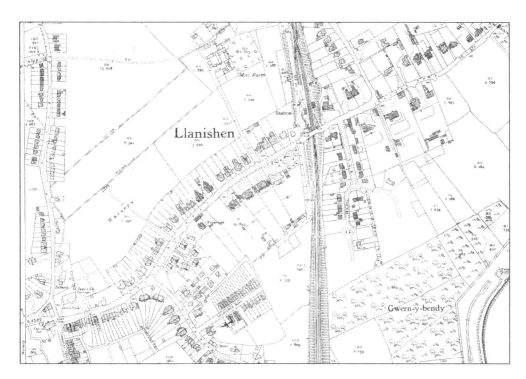

Llanishen has become much more urbanised since this map of the village was compiled in 1940. Part of the reservoir can be seen in the bottom right corner and Heol Hir is now the main road leading to the Thornhill housing estate.

Llanishen is named after St Isan who founded a Christian community in the sixth century, where the Oval in Llandennis Road is now situated. According to tradition, he established a wattle and daub church at this site, where the spring and the burial mound used by the monks is still visible. In 1993 the Llanishen Historical Society planted a tree to mark the settlement.

After the Norman Conquest, the Augustinian abbey of Keynsham was awarded land in Llanishen as part of its estates in and around Cardiff. Another beneficiary was Tewkesbury Abbey, the favourite ecclesiastical endowment of Robert Fitzhamon. He allowed the abbey to establish St Mary's Church and Priory in Cardiff and the church in Llanishen was built as one of its outlying chapels. It served worshippers in the tiny hamlet but it was Tewkesbury Abbey that reaped most of the benefit from its tithes.

The Normans built the present St Isan's Church, which probably dates from the middle of the 12th century. It was described in 1860 as 'a neat little structure in the English style of architecture with a whitewashed interior and a fine pointed chancel arch'. In 1872 the capacity of the church was enlarged and most of its stained glass dates from this time.

This view of St Isan's Church from Station Road was taken soon after its restoration in 1872.

Following the Dissolution of the Monasteries, St Isan's became the parish church of Llanishen. The monastic property was distributed among a number of the leading local gentry, including the Kemys family of Cefn Mably and Edward Lewis of the Van near Caerphilly. The original home of the Lewises was near the church at Llanishen House but in the 18th century they moved to New House, a splendid mansion on Thornhill which is now a hotel. The Lewis family were to exercise a benevolent influence on the village. Among their charitable works were the building and maintenance of the almshouses, which for many years stood opposite the church.

The famous Cromwell family also has a local connection. Richard Williams, who was born in Llanishen, was the nephew of Thomas Cromwell. His influence as Lord Chancellor to Henry VIII enabled Richard to prosper. In 1536 Richard changed his name to Cromwell and soon afterwards he was appointed South Wales Commissioner for the Suppression of the Monasteries. He was knighted and granted church lands in Huntingdonshire which he exchanged for lands in Neath and other parts of Glamorgan. The legal documents refer to him as, 'Richard Williams, alias Cromwell'. He became MP for Huntingdon and his grandson was Oliver Cromwell.

When the Rhymney Railway built its direct line to Cardiff in 1872 by tunnelling through Caerphilly Mountain, it passed through Llanishen and many of the navvies lived in huts along the line. The construction of this link was not without its

Llanishen Fach in Heol Erwin actually lies just across the modern boundary of Llanishen in the suburb of Rhiwbina. The house is believed to be the seat of the influential Williams family, the ancestors of Oliver Cromwell, and a street nearby is named 'Clos Cromwell'.

Station Road, 1912. St Isan's Church is on the right and the Church Inn is facing us. As this busy road now passes through the main shopping centre of Llanishen, mothers no longer venture forth with their prams in the middle of the road.

The Llanishen and Lisvane reservoirs from Caerphilly Mountain. Though no longer a source of water for Cardiff, the reservoirs are regarded as an important amenity for leisure and recreation. Plans to develop the site are meeting with strong opposition.

tragedies, as several of the workers were killed and lie buried in Llanishen churchyard.

Many of the farms at that time bore names still familiar in the district, such as Fidlas, Ty-Glas, Llanishen Fach and Heol Hir. There were only a few roads leading to the village, where the most important buildings, apart from the church, were the Church Inn, the blacksmith's forge and the little National school which had opened in 1867. This school was built on land donated by the Marquis of Bute and served the community for a hundred years. It has now been converted into the church hall.

At the rear of Fidlas Farm were Llanishen and Lisvane reservoirs. A severe drought in 1887 had reduced Cardiff's water supply to only 14 days and the 60 acres of water at Llanishen was completed just in time to avoid a crisis. Even though much larger reservoirs were later built in the Brecon Beacons, Llanishen and Lisvane remained an important source of water for many years. They also became popular, both for their pleasant environment and as a venue for water sports. When the American owners of the reservoir, Western Power Distribution, recently released plans to build luxury homes on the site, it was not surprising that local people should be horrified at proposals to change a site of considerable beauty.

The large, solidly built houses in Station Road began to appear in the 1880s. Just before World War One, Lt-Col. Frank Gaskell, whose father was chairman of Hancock's Brewery, lived at Boscobel near the modern police station. He was an

officer in the Boer War and then practised as a barrister till the outbreak of war in 1914. He served with the Welsh Regiment and, after being shot in the jaw, he was invalided home. He played a leading role in raising the 16th Cardiff City Battalion before returning to active service, only to break his leg in a riding accident. Once more this brave man returned to the conflict and on 16 May 1916 he was mortally wounded when an enemy bullet struck his ammunition pouch. He was buried at Merville Cemetery and memorials, both at St Isan's Church and St John's in the centre of Cardiff, honour his courage.

T.H. Ensor, who also lived in Station Road, is remembered for a different reason. In a letter to the *Western Mail*, Ensor made many scurrilous remarks about John Batchelor, a former Mayor of Cardiff who died in 1883. Among his more charitable comments were: 'Traitor to the Crown ... sincerely mourned by unpaid creditors ... a demagogue and a pauper'. Batchelor's friends sued Ensor and the editor of the *Western Mail* for libel. The case became famous in legal history, as both were acquitted on the grounds that 'the dead have no rights and suffer no wrongs'.

Bishop Hedley lived at the house now occupied by the Court School, where his private chapel can still be seen. An ardent believer in education, he did much to promote Catholic schools in Cardiff but is remembered primarily for his part in the opening of Catholic halls of residence at Oxford and Cambridge Universities.

In 1910 Fidlas Road was narrower than it is today and its houses had large front gardens. These have since become much reduced as this busy road has been widened. Near the viaduct, the tiny Bridge Cottage is 300 years old and measures no more

This photograph of the early 20th century shows the fine Victorian houses in Station Road, which were among the earliest to be built in Llanishen.

than 24 feet by 18, though it has a large garden hidden from the road. The friendly ghosts of a red-haired girl and a white horse supposedly haunt the building.

When Llanishen became a suburb of Cardiff in 1922, it was several years before it lost its village atmosphere. There had never been much industry in the district apart from the Llanishen Brick Works. In 1890 the factory was producing 100,000 bricks a week, in addition to terracotta goods which were said to be very artistic. By 1900 the works had disappeared to make way for the construction of Llandennis Road and the Oval.

The first major industrial site in Llanishen was built in 1939, when a site of 47 acres was chosen in Caerphilly Road as a Royal Ordnance Factory. Manufacturing began a year later and, during the war, ROF Llanishen produced anti-aircraft guns, pontoon couplings and aircraft cannon. Priority was given to tank and anti-tank guns and in a single month in 1944 the works produced 1,784 tank guns, a record for any factory in the British Empire. The works suffered a tragic incident on 27 March 1943, when a shell from one of the anti-aircraft batteries exploded and killed nine people.

Bridge Cottage is one of the oldest buildings in the district and the sole survivor of nine such dwellings that once encircled St Isan's Church.

After World War Two, the factory turned to civilian activities for a time before resuming armaments production. It entered its most contentious period when it became the Atomic Weapons Establishment and attracted the attention of the CND movement. There was a scare in 1993 when someone hurled a suitcase, later detonated by a controlled explosion, at the security gates. The position of such a

high-risk plant in a suburban area contributed to its closure. The site has now been levelled and decontaminated in readiness for a new and more peaceful purpose.

In the last half century Llanishen has experienced radical change. Ty-Glas Road and Ty-Glas Avenue have become a dividing line between housing and commercial development. South of that line, apart from a small housing estate around Fishguard Road, the area has been used to build the Inland Revenue Offices, a number of superstores and the Ty-Glas Industrial Estate and Business Park. North of Ty-Glas Road, a massive building programme of private and council houses has been undertaken. This surge of modern housing began in the 1950s and, despite plans to use former industrial sites such as that of the Phoenix Brickworks, it has continued through the greenery of Thornhill almost to Caerphilly Mountain. As a result, open spaces in Llanishen, other than the reservoirs, are now at a premium.

Field gun production at ROF Llanishen in World War Two. After the war, the factory's involvement in nuclear weapons aroused controversy but the plant was not closed until the 1990s.

Further Reading:

Horton, G. *Llanishen from Village to Suburb*, Llanishen Local History Society, 1999.

LLANRUMNEY

Population: 12,200

After the Norman Conquest, Llanrumney was among the lands bequeathed to Keynsham Abbey by the Lord of Glamorgan. The monks built a small chapel where Llanrumney Hall now stands and, following the Dissolution of the Monasteries, the

Llanrumney in 1901 was still a peaceful country district, where the route of Ball Road is similar to that of today. Llanrumney Hall, Ball House, Mill farmhouse and Fishpond Wood are recognisable landmarks on the modern estate.

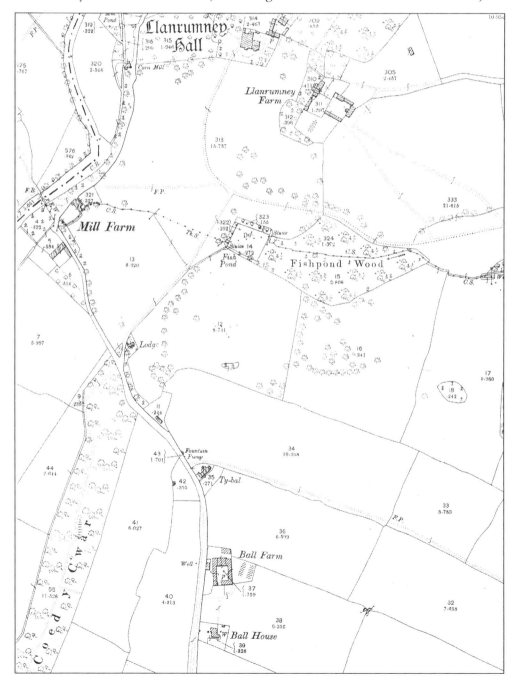

estate passed into the hands of the Kemys family. Until the 20th century, there were few buildings of significance in the area but the most important of these was Llanrumney Hall.

In 1560 William Kemys left the property to his daughter, who married Thomas Morgan. The Morgan coat-of-arms, dated 1587, can be seen above a fireplace at the hall, where five generations of the family lived. Many of them are buried in the Llanrumney Chapel of St Mellons Church.

There are a number of interesting legends relating to Llanrumney Hall. One unlikely tale concerns the Welsh Prince, Llywelyn ap Gruffydd, who was slain at Builth Wells in 1282. Supposedly, his head was presented to Edward I at Conway, but the rest of the body was brought by monks to Llanrumney and interred in a stone coffin. The story has never been confirmed, despite claims that the coffin was discovered within the thicker walls of the house in the early 19th century. There have also been reports from some quarters that the headless body of Llywelyn has appeared as a ghost.

Much more plausible is the belief that Sir Henry Morgan, who became the most famous pirate to terrorise the Spanish Main, was born at Llanrumney Hall in around 1635. Details of his early life are somewhat shadowy but, after leaving Llanrumney, Morgan joined a ship bound for Barbados. There he was sold as an indentured servant and, after serving his time, found congenial company with a band of buccaneers in Jamaica. In 1668 he became their leader and three years later he carried out his most daring exploit, when he captured Panama and broke Spanish

Llanrumney Hall in the 1890s, when it was still owned by the Williams family. According to legend, this was the burial place of Llywelyn ap Gruffydd and the birthplace of Henry Morgan.

Another view of the hall, as the Tredegar Hunt assembles for a day's sport in the 1920s.

power in the Caribbean. Morgan was a brave and intrepid leader but he was also cruel and treacherous. He even cheated his men out of their share of the booty taken from Panama. Morgan's piratical deeds came to an end in 1672, when he was arrested and sent back to England for trial. However, there had been an ambivalent attitude towards privateering since Elizabethan times and the famous diarist, John Evelyn, expressed the views of many in his comments on the sacking of Panama: 'Such an action had not been done since the famous Drake'. Morgan certainly convinced Charles II of his worth and not only did he return to Jamaica as its Deputy Governor, but he was also given a knighthood. Ironically he then tried to stamp out piracy in the Caribbean and died a wealthy man in 1688. One of the Jamaican properties left by Henry Morgan to his wife was named 'Llanrumney'.

In the early 20th century, C.C. Williams became the last lord of the manor at Llanrumney Hall. Known as Squire Williams, he was a typical country gentleman and a much-respected local figure. His 700 acres of rich farmland, woods and a small lake offered 'a charming sylvan setting' to his home. Williams loved the countryside and was a keen sportsman who once played cricket at Lords against W.G. Grace. He was Master of the Tredegar Hunt, Sheriff of Monmouthshire in 1925 and in World War One he was awarded the Military Cross.

C.C. Williams remained the leader of this agricultural community which until 1951 was in the county of Monmouthshire. In that year Llanrumney Hall and its parkland were sold by compulsory purchase to Cardiff City Council. Squire Williams could have remained at the hall but, saddened at the loss of his lands, he moved to the Vale of Glamorgan. A few years later Llanrumney Hall was sold to Hancocks' Brewery and was converted into a public house.

The land was needed to provide new homes for 12,000 people and, while most of them were council houses, there were private properties as well, some of which stand at the top of the hill in Ball Road. The old houses of Ball Farm and Mill Farm have been absorbed into the modern estate, kindling memories of the past. Some of the original flats in Ball Road were unsightly and have been demolished, but generally the estate was attractively designed. There are several open spaces, including a 21-acre playing field separating Newport Road from the housing estate. Many of the trees were preserved and the open parkland surrounding Llanrumney Hall provides a pleasing aspect to this historic building.

Llanrumney from Glastonbury Terrace, 2002. The parkland around the hall bears testimony to the careful planning of this housing estate.

Further Reading: Bielski, A. *The Story of St Mellons*, Alun Books, 1985

Ball House, now set among modern housing along Ball Road, arouses memories of Llanrumney's rural past.

OLD ST MELLONS
AND PONTPRENNAU

Population: 7,650

The village of St Mellons has not greatly changed since this map of 1940 and familiar landmarks are the church, the White Hart and Quarry Hill. However, the fields to the left of Newport Road are now part of the Llanrumney estate.

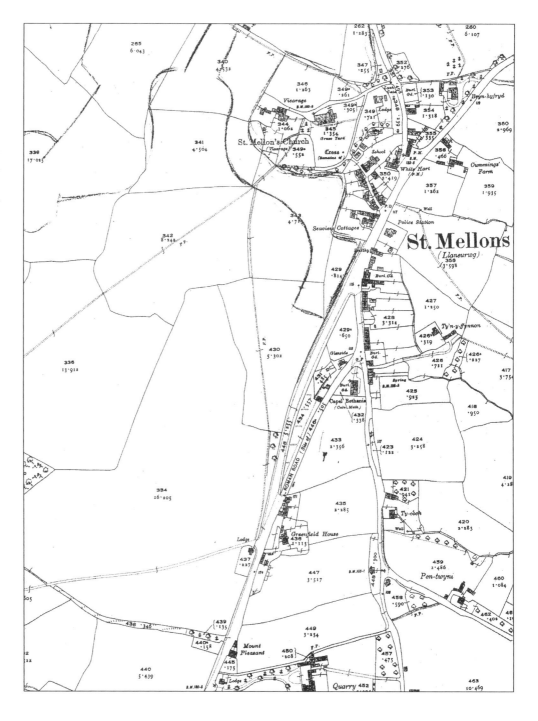

St Mellons Church from the east. The present building dates from about 1360, when it was rebuilt in the Decorated Perpendicular style.

Historic Cefn Mably was the home of the Kemys-Tynte family until 1920. Later it became a hospital and has now been converted into elegant apartments.

Old St Mellons and Pontprennau is an electoral division in the north-east of Cardiff. Prehistoric finds have been discovered near Druidstone House, where the Silures had an open-air temple in the shape of a cromlech. Two of the original stones were broken up for road repairs in the 19th century but one survives as a mantelpiece in the house.

Llaneurwg, as St Mellons is known in Welsh, is named after a Welsh chief of the second century. According to tradition, he requested the Pope to send missionaries to his domain and, after being baptised in the River Rhymney, Eurwg and his people built a wattle church. When the Normans conquered the region, they dedicated a new church to St Mellon, their patron saint. Mellon is buried at Rouen Cathedral, where the archives claim that he was born into a noble family at Cardiola, assumed by some to be Cardiff. After visiting Rome, where he was converted to Christianity, Mellon brought the Christian message to Rouen and became its bishop.

The Norman church at St Mellons was completely rebuilt and extended in the 14th century. Its size indicates that it was intended to reflect the glory of God, though the community at that time was quite small. The church still bears many of its mediaeval features, including the font, a stoup for holy water and evidence of a rood loft.

For hundreds of years, Cefn Mably or Mabel's Ridge was the home of the principal family in this part of South Wales. Mabel was the daughter of Robert Fitzhamon and she built a house or a hunting lodge on the site of a later mansion. The lords of Glamorgan held the estate until the early 13th century, when Cefn Mably passed into the possession of Stephen de Kemys, thus beginning an association with St Mellons and the surrounding parishes for the next 800 years. The Kemys family were not only the biggest landowners in the region but also its

Quarry Hill, seen here in 1920, ceased to be the residence of the Cope family in 1948. It is now used by Southern Cross Health Care as a nursing home.

political leaders. Between 1576 and 1783 they provided nine sheriffs of Glamorgan and several MPs for Monmouthshire.

Not surprisingly, Sir Nicholas Kemys and his son, Charles, fought for the King during the Civil War. In 1646 Charles joined other Royalists to attack the Round-head garrison at Cardiff Castle and, as Parliament forces came to its relief, a running battle took place towards Cefn Mably which came under siege. When the war ended, Charles was fined £3,500 and sent into exile for two years. He was more fortunate than Nicholas who was killed while heroically defending Chepstow Castle for the King.

Cefn Mably was a splendid house set in 6,000 acres of beautiful countryside, within which roamed a large herd of deer. When the house was rebuilt in the 16th century by Lewis Kemys, the dining room was beautifully panelled in oak and had a secret hiding place behind a large picture. In the Soldiers' Gallery, probably given its name after a garrison was quartered there during the siege of 1646, there was a long refectory table, 52 feet in length. An eastern wing and a new chapel were added in the 18th century.

Cefn Mably was sold in 1920 and four years later it became a hospital for the treatment of tuberculosis. From 1948 until 1983 it continued to be used as a hospital within the National Health Service. Cefn Mably then became vacant for 15 years and during this time it was gutted by fire. In recent years Meadgate Homes have tastefully restored the house and converted it into luxury apartments. The development also includes mews cottages and houses in Cefn Mably Park.

The Blue Bell in 1906. The offer of 'good stabling' is an indication that the horse was still a vital form of transport at this time.

These children are posing for the camera in 1914. Behind them, in the centre, is the Fox and Hounds Hotel and on the hill is St Mellons Church.

Quarry Hill was another fine property, built in the Georgian style for the Cope family. The altar oak screen in St Mellons Church was a family gift, erected by Matthew Cope in 1918 to the memory of his wife, Margaret. Local people had a great affection for her and she was looked upon as, 'the good angel and lady bountiful of St Mellons for half a century'. Their son, Willie Cope, became MP for Llandaff and Barry and the glass in the east window of the church was given by him in memory of his parents. During World War One, Major Willie was the chairman of the recruiting committee as 181 men from St Mellons went to war. The memorial near the Fox and Hounds indicates that 23 did not return.

Before the Reformation, the annual St Mellons Fair was organised by the monks of the monastery at Llanrumney. The chief event was a race from the monastery to St Mellons Church. The winner was awarded the sanctus bell, which he returned to the monks in time for the next service. According to a legend, the bell had a blue clapper and the inn near the finishing post is appropriately named the Bluebell. The fair was held on 22 October, St Mellon's Day, and continued until 1859, when a disturbance involved rivals from Castleton who were holding their own fair at the same time. The fair was replaced by a ploughing match which evolved into the St Mellons Show. This was held at Llanrumney Park until the modern housing estate was built and is now a popular annual event at Tredegar House.

Another tradition was the Shrove Tuesday football match with Rumney. The goals were the respective churches of the two villages. The ball could be kicked or carried and anyone could take part if they were prepared to risk a few broken bones.

In 1794 a Rumney player died when his skull was fractured and the fixture was discontinued for several years. The prize for the victors was a free sampling of the beaten village's favourite tipple. In St Mellons they had a choice of pubs at either the White Hart, the Bluebell or the Fox and Hounds.

The local churches have always played an important role in the village life of St Mellons. By the early 19th century there were Baptist and Methodist chapels, while a Welsh Independent Chapel was later converted into an educational centre. It was opened by the Prince of Wales in 1921 and for many years it was a meeting place for youth activities and adult education. In 1854 the Poor House was purchased by the Church for the princely sum of 2s 6d and converted into the village school. It served this purpose until the 1980s, when the school moved to modern premises in Llanrumney.

St Mellons became a suburb of Cardiff in 1974 and has recently been joined by Pontprennau, which translates into English as: 'the bridge of the trees'. Once just another farm in the parish of Llanedeyrn, it is now a rapidly growing housing estate. New houses have also been built in Old St Mellons near Eastern Avenue and many would argue that the village has been spoilt by so much urban encroachment. Yet the countryside is still not far away. The St Mellons Country Club and Hotel, set in spacious grounds, is an eagerly sought venue for wedding receptions and social events, while members of the local golf club enjoy one of the most attractive courses in the Cardiff area.

To meet the ever increasing demand for accomodation in Cardiff, Pontprennau Farm has been transformed into a 'greenfield' housing estate.

Further Reading:
Bielski, A. *The Story of St Mellons*, Alun Books, 1985

PENTYRCH AND CREIGIAU

Population: 7,230

The parish of Pentyrch, which includes the hamlets of Creigiau and Gwaelod-y-Garth, was first inhabited more than 3,000 years ago. Bronze Age burial mounds on the Garth Mountain, a cromlech in Creigiau, together with tools and bones discovered in the Lesser Garth Cave, are evidence of the time when Neolithic and Bronze Age farmers scratched a living from the light upland soil.

When St Cadoc of Llancarfan entered this lonely valley in the sixth century, he found a small community clustered around a 'magic well', now known as Ffynnon Catwg. For many years it was the only source of water in the village and Cadoc built his church near this well. St Catwg's has been rebuilt from time to time and the present Victorian Gothic church replaced a simple structure consisting of a nave and chancel.

The powerful Mathew family began to exert their influence over Pentyrch in the 15th century. One branch of the family lived in Creigiau where Robert ap Mathew built Castell-y-Mynach. Eleven generations of the Mathew family lived there from the 15th to the 18th century, though initially the lands they held in the district were modest. It was their more wealthy kinsmen in Radyr who built up an estate in Pentyrch and established a profitable iron industry.

Initially, the works produced plate iron but Edmund Mathew courted controversy when he turned his attention to the manufacturing of cannon and became involved in gun-running. The works produced cannon of a high quality but profits were jeopardised when an embargo was placed on exports, as England's relations with Spain deteriorated. In 1574 Edmund was accused by the Privy Council of illegally exporting guns from Cardiff. He weathered that storm but, untroubled by patriotic scruples, continued his illicit trade.

In 1602 the Privy Council again voiced its concern, ordering 'that especiall care be had to put down Edmund Mathew esq., for casting any ordnance at his furnace near Cardiff, because from that place very easily it may be carried into Spain'. Between 1582 and 1600, as the 'port officers were poor and dared not displease him', Mathew illegally exported 150 tons of ordnance from Cardiff

By the early 17th century, Edmund was in financial difficulties and leased his works to a kindred spirit, Peter Semayne. As late as 1614 the Privy Council was still accusing Semayne of 'arming all the world with our artillery against us', but on this

occasion action was taken and the furnace destroyed. In 1625 the Mathews of Radyr sold their lands in Pentyrch and now it was the turn of the Castell-y-Mynach branch of the family to prosper.

Thomas Mathew was Sheriff of Glamorgan in 1613 and, taking advantage of his office, he added considerably to his estate. Known as 'Mathew Tew', he was a bully who terrorised the area. He appeared before the Star Chamber and was accused of 'perjury … use of false measures in buying barley … refusal to licence ale houses that did not sell his ale … other misconduct in office'. Some might say that the painful death he suffered was justice. According to legend, he sat on a shoemaker's awl placed under the cushion of a bench where he always sat. It had been put there by a cottager bearing a grudge and until recently the bench was preserved. Cecil Mathew was the last member of the family to live at Castell-y-Mynach and, when she died in 1720, the estate passed to her husband, Lord Talbot of Hensol.

Though agriculture was the basis of the local economy, Nicholas Price from Caer-philly and Thomas Lewis from Llanishen leased land from Lord Talbot in 1740 to re-establish the iron industry in Pentyrch. Drift mines in the area provided high-quality steam coal, nearby quarries produced limestone and there was an abundance of timber. Iron ore was transported to the furnaces by pack mules and donkeys from the mines in Little Garth and Fforest Goch. As the population increased, most of the

For 1,500 years St Catwg's Church has stood on this site. The present building dates from 1857 and its spire bears the familiar style of its architects, John Prichard and J.P. Seddon.

Contrary to its name, Castell-y-Mynach was neither a castle nor a monastery. The east wing to the right is the oldest part of the present house.

The old furnace at Pentyrch, looking across the river to Taff's Well. This site is now a housing estate.

miners and iron workers lived in or around Gwaelod-y-Garth, formerly known as 'Lower Pentyrch', while the farming community centred around the old village and Creigiau.

The farm, from which Creigiau takes its name, looks rather isolated in this view dating from around 1900. At that time the village was still in its early stages of development.

A bright future appeared to beckon, as production trebled between 1829 and 1846, following a merger with the Melingriffith Company in Whitchurch. However, the Pentyrch works declined as it lacked the capital to compete with steel produced by the Bessemer process. After a bitter strike, workers accepted a 10 percent cut in wages which caused severe hardship and only delayed the inevitable. By 1888 the furnaces of Pentyrch had closed and now the only industry found in the district is quarrying.

Until 1896, Creigiau, named after Criga Farm, was virtually unknown apart from its limestone quarries. When the Barry Railway Company built a station, the district became popular with ramblers and cyclists and soon Creigiau was being hailed as one of the healthiest places in Glamorgan. 'Everyone who goes to those beautiful slopes below Pentyrch comes away singing its praises', wrote a *South Wales Echo* reporter in 1901.

An American military hospital was built at Rhydlafar during World War Two, in preparation for the casualties expected after the Normandy landings. Trainloads of

Rhydlafar Hospital shortly before its closure. Built to accommodate wounded American servicemen, the hospital later performed an important role for the NHS.

American soldiers, some with horrific injuries, were brought to Creigiau Station where they were met by volunteer ambulance drivers, usually women, who transported them to the hospital. After the war, Rhydlafar served the National Health Service for many years. The hospital was recently demolished and a housing estate is now being built on the site.

Welsh remained the first language for most people in Pentyrch until the 1920s and even now the district has a higher proportion of Welsh speakers than elsewhere in Cardiff. When Pentyrch became the city's newest suburb in 1996, the boundaries of Cardiff reached the edge of the coalfield on which its prosperity was based. Yet Pentyrch and Creigiau still have a rural appearance and there are few scars from its industrial past. The population is rapidly rising, as the district acts as a dormitory suburb for Cardiff and Pontypridd, and the extensive housing developments of the last 20 years suggest that the countryside separating Pentyrch from the city may soon be a thing of the past.

Further Reading:
Pentyrch and District Local History Society, *Pentyrch, Creigiau and Gwaelod-y-Garth,* Chalford Publishing Company, 1997
Davies, J.B. *The Parish of Pentyrch* in Glamorgan Historian Vol. I, Stewart Williams, 1963

St Catwg's Church is at the heart of the 'old village' in this postcard of Pentyrch, c.1900. The former vicarage lies just to its right.

PENYLAN

Population: 12,570

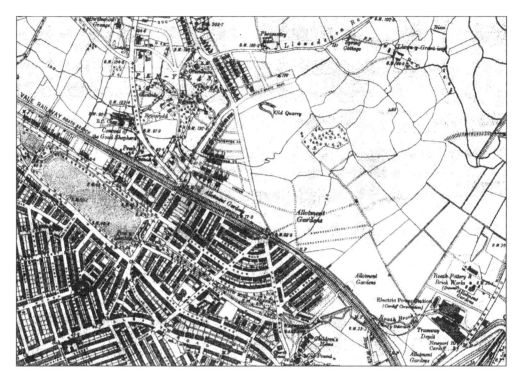

Penylan, meaning 'the summit', lies within the parish of Roath which became a part of Cardiff in 1875. The oldest indication of man's presence in South Wales was discovered at an allotment site on Penylan Hill in 1953. It was a quartzite hand axe, estimated to be between 75,000 and 250,000 years old. A Palaeolithic nomad, of whom there were probably no more than 50 in the whole of Wales at that time, probably mislaid it while he was out hunting for game.

After the Norman Conquest, Keynsham Abbey became the principal beneficiary in Penylan, when it was granted an estate north of Roath Brook between Penylan Hill and the River Rhymney. Until the 20th century Penylan Hill, or 'Welshman's Hill' as it was better known, was no more than a track leading to Cyncoed. Along the way were a number of wells, visited by people on church feast days. These visitors would take the water home, believing in its healing qualities. Some left coins or religious medallions in the wells as an offering.

St Margaret's, the parish church of Roath, is first mentioned in the 12th century when it was a chapel of Tewkesbury Abbey. This simple, whitewashed building, with its single bell turret, became the parish church after the Reformation and served the small community of Roath for 700 years. The 1st Marquis of Bute purchased the living of St Margaret's in 1793 and seven years later, at the time of his first wife's death, he built a family vault to the north of the chancel.

When the church was demolished in 1868, the vault was reconstructed as an ornate mausoleum, dominated by seven sarcophagi in red granite, not unlike those containing the Tsars in St Petersburg. Among the members of the Bute family buried in the vault are the 1st Marquis, his two wives and his eldest son. The mausoleum was incorporated into a new St Margaret's Church, designed by John Prichard and opened in July 1870. He employed a variety of building materials in his work which was praised by *The Architect* for 'the rich effect produced by the harmonising contrasts of coloured stone which distinguish the church as one of the most beautifully-finished in the principality'.

After the Dissolution of the Monasteries, the Keynsham lands in Penylan passed into the possession of the Morgan family of Tredegar House. For the next 350 years the district remained agricultural with farms such as Ty-Gwyn, Deri, Ty-Mawr and Roath Court concentrating mainly on pastoral farming.

When Roath became a suburb of Cardiff, these farms began to disappear, as the growing population of the borough sought new homes. In the late 19th century, magnificent houses were built on the site of Penylan Farm in Ty-Gwyn Road and Penylan Road, though most of them no longer exist. Bronwydd was a large villa built for Daniel Thomas, a successful public works engineer. It survived until 1970, when it was bulldozed to make way for Eastern Avenue. William Young, a wealthy

Old St Margaret's Church with the Bute Vault on its left. The Early English style of architecture is shown in the windows and the west door.

Birchwood Grange, off Ty-Gwyn Road, was built in 1890 for Sir Charles James Jackson. He was an architect, a barrister and one time chairman of The News of the World.

Next page: The Lady Mary Estate in 1960, eight years before the railway line was closed. The gardens of Roath Park are at the foot of the photograph, with Fairoak Farm to the right of the houses on Lake Road East. At the top are the cooling towers in Colchester Avenue.

potato merchant, lived at Oldwell and in the 1960s it became an old people's home. In 1987 it was demolished to make way for the housing association flats at Redwell Court. Penylan Farm House became part of the Convent of the Good Shepherd, built by the 3rd Marquis of Bute in 1872 for 'fallen women'. St David's Sixth-Form College now stands on this site. One house which still survives is Birchwood Grange. It was once the residence of Sir Charles Jackson but now serves as a university hall of residence.

By 1914, well-built town houses lined Penylan Hill, Waterloo Road and many of the streets linking them. Some of these roads bear the names of battles such as Kimberley, Mafeking, Blenheim and Trafalgar. Balaclava Road and Alma Road recall the famous events in which Godfrey Morgan, the 2nd Viscount Tredegar, was involved. During the Crimean War, he served with the 17th Lancers and took part in the terrifying Charge of the Light Brigade, immortalised by Lord Tennyson. Of the 673 lancers who charged the Russian guns, less than a third survived. Tredegar later described how his horse, Sir Briggs, despite being wounded by a sabre, safely carried him back to the British lines.

Lord Tredegar was renowned for his generosity. He offered five acres of land towards the creation of Roath Park, but his most attractive legacy in Penylan is Waterloo Gardens and Mill Gardens, which resulted in a beautiful stretch of greenery from Penylan Road to St Margaret's Church. The Harlequins Recreation Ground near Newport Road, which is still in use today, was also sited on Tredegar land.

Lord Tredegar gave the land on which the beautiful Waterloo Gardens were laid out. Along the skyline, in the centre, is the present St Margaret's Church.

The Roath Power Station in Newport Road began supplying electricity in 1902, the same year in which electric trams, the foundation of Cardiff's transport system until 1950, were delivered to a depot next door. These landmarks and others have gone, including the cooling towers in Colchester Avenue which dominated the skyline until their demolition in 1972. Their place has been taken by workshops and small factories on the Colchester Trading Estate, while Newport Road is now lined with garages, depots and superstores.

The earliest houses in Colchester Avenue were built in 1912, when open fields separated them from the industrial development of Newport Road. After World War Two a new housing estate sprang up in this part of Penylan. About the same time, the Howardian and Lady Margaret high schools were built in Colchester Avenue to replace the school in Adamsdown which had been damaged in the Blitz. When these schools closed in 1990, this site too was allocated to housing and many of the roads are named after former teachers.

The Lady Mary Estate of solid well-built houses was created in the 1950s on land once occupied by Fairoak Farm. Within this residential area, the synagogue in Arnside Road became the principal place of worship for the Jewish community in Cardiff. Recently the number of Jews in Cardiff has declined and a smaller

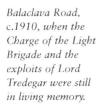

Balaclava Road, c.1910, when the Charge of the Light Brigade and the exploits of Lord Tredegar were still in living memory.

synagogue, together with new homes, is being constructed in Cyncoed Road at the former Penylan Gardens.

Further Reading:
Childs, J. *Roath, Splott and Adamsdown*, Chalford Publishing Company, 1995

PLASNEWYDD

Population: 17,190

Roath Dogfield was the name given to the manor retained by the Lord of Glamorgan after the Norman Conquest and today most of that district is in the electoral division of Plasnewydd. The village of Roath grew around the manor house at Roath Court. This ancient site, where a circular mound is surrounded by a ditch, suggests that it may have been an administrative centre for the early Welsh rulers of Cibwr. The present building dates back to the 18th century but in 1578 Rice Merrick mentions an earlier manor house, fortified and moated, 'which is called The Court, but now in ruin'.

Dairy farming was the principal activity of the mediaeval manor. The land was originally worked by serfs who gave their labour at certain times of the year as rent for the land they held. By the early 14th century most of the tenants at the manor were free men and, after the carnage of the Black Death, feudal service was virtually eliminated.

Not far from the manor house was the lord's mill. It was powered by water from the stream which still flows through Waterloo Gardens and by 1316 was acting as

Roath Court, 1826, painted by an unknown artist soon after the Williams family had purchased the property.

Roath Mill in 1897, shortly before its demolition. A document of 1314, referring to the earlier mill on the site, records that a lease was granted to Richard Tucker 'to hold for the term of his life'.

a fulling mill for local weavers. Roath Mill was rebuilt in the 18th century and remained in use until 1897, when it was demolished to make way for new houses.

Though the Marquis of Bute was the Lord of Roath Manor, the Williams family became the owners of Roath Court in 1824 and lived there until 1952. The most notable resident in this period was Charles Croft Williams who was an alderman, several times Mayor of Cardiff and also Master of the Glamorgan Hunt. In 1952 the property became a funeral home when it was purchased by Morlais Summers.

Lord Tredegar was another prominent landowner in Plasnewydd and, from the 1850s onwards, fine houses were built on his land. The district around The Parade, The Walk, East Grove and West Grove became known as Tredegarville and of particular interest are two houses built by James Howell, the Cardiff store owner. Each of them became the offical residence of the Lord Mayor of Cardiff. Howell's first home at The Walk has since been converted into flats, but the present Mansion House has a fine double-bay frontage and was originally intended to be two separate dwellings for his sons. They chose not to live there and, when their father died in 1909, the house was sold to the council. Its spacious, pleasant rooms make it an ideal setting for the Lord Mayor to receive distinguished visitors.

Not far away in Newport Road, Cardiff's first infirmary was opened in 1837. Money was raised from a number of sources. Daniel Jones, a wealthy lawyer from

Beaupre, donated £3,500, the Marquis of Bute gave a further £1,000 and all the money raised at the Cardiff Eisteddfod of 1834 was given to the cause. The Glamorgan and Monmouthshire Infirmary was able to accommodate about 30 patients and was extended in 1866. Even so, by 1880 its resources were strained to the limit and it was decided to build a new infirmary at Longcross.

The former hospital then became the first campus of the new University of Wales College at Cardiff which, in its first year, provided courses in the arts and sciences for 109 men and 42 women. The number of students grew rapidly and in 1909 the university moved to Cathays Park. The old premises remained in use and after World War One were greatly enlarged to house the Welsh School of Medicine. The original infirmary building was demolished in 1966 and five years later the school was transferred to the Heath Hospital. The site in Newport Road is now used by the Engineering Department of the university.

Roath Castle, so called because of its crenellated battlements, was the home of the Richards family. Arabella was the posthumous daughter of Edward Richards who was tragically killed in 1858, when his horse collided with a cartload of manure in Newport Road. She inherited his estate and married Donald Mackintosh of Mackintosh, the wealthy leader of the Scottish clan. The development of their property in Roath began soon after their marriage and many of the new streets, such as Arabella, Donald, Diana, Angus, Alfred and Mackintosh, were named after the

James Howell commissioned this splendid building in Westgrove which subsequently became the Mansion House and residence of the Lord Mayor of Cardiff.

The old Cardiff Infirmary in Newport Road, c.1874. Nine years later it became the first home of the University College of South Wales and Monmouthshire.

Plasnewydd Mansion, more commonly known as Roath Castle, c.1880. The garden later became the bowling green of the Mackintosh Institute.

family. The association with Scotland is also commemorated by Keppoch Street, Inverness Place and Strathnairn Street. In 1890, 10 years after their marriage, Arabella donated Roath Castle to her tenants. It was renamed the Mackintosh Institute and is still used as a community centre. Among its facilities is a beautiful bowling green on which the famous cricketer W.G. Grace once played.

The splendid houses in Ninian Road, opposite Roath Park, were built on land owned by the Butes. The road is named after Lord Ninian Stuart, MP for Cardiff before World War One and son of the 3rd Marquis. A popular figure in Cardiff, he was killed by a sniper at the Battle of Loos in 1915. A statue stands to his memory in Cathays Park.

Castle Road became City Road in 1905 to celebrate Cardiff's new status but, before urban development began in 1873, it was known as Plwcca Lane leading to Plwcca Halog, the Gallows Field. Two Roman Catholic priests were hung, drawn and quartered at this sinister spot where five roads now meet. Philip Evans and John Lloyd were caught up in the hysteria of the Popish Plot, a fantastic falsehood which alleged that the Pope was planning to invade England and replace Charles II with his Catholic brother, James. The death penalty was automatically applied to Jesuit priests and Philip Evans's final words were: 'If I had ever so many lives, I would willingly give them all for so good a cause'. A stained-glass window was later dedicated to the martyrs at St Peter's Roman Catholic Church.

In the mid-19th century Merthyr Road was a country lane, constructed after the Heath Enclosure Act. Its name was changed to Albany Road in 1884 in memory of

The site of the Gallows Field. A plaque on the wall of the National Westminster Bank in Crwys Road commemorates the martyrdom of Philip Evans and John Lloyd in 1679.

the Duke of Albany. Building began that same year and 117 shops were established on the road by 1914. Plasnewydd has changed little since that time and in this densely populated suburb, City Road, Albany Road and Wellfield Road are among the busiest shopping centres in Cardiff.

Further Reading:

Childs, J. *Roath, Splott and Adamsdown*, Chalford Publishing Company, 1995

The Rhymney Station has gone and streets have replaced the open land behind Roath Court. Otherwise Plasnewydd, lying to the north of Newport Road, has seen few changes since this map was produced in 1922.

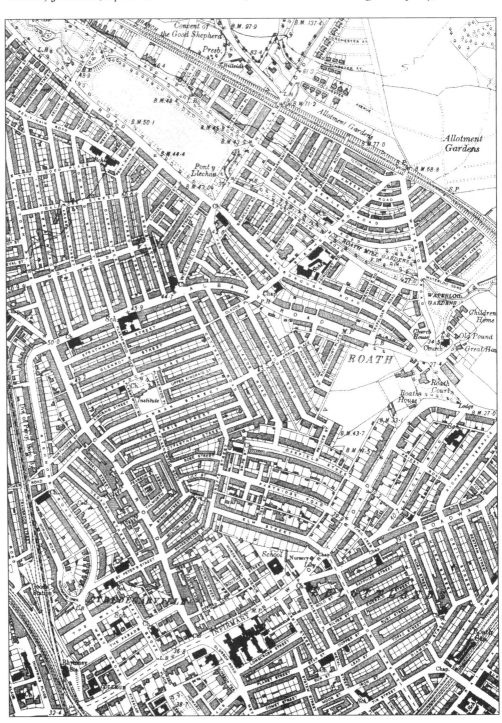

RADYR AND MORGANSTOWN

Population: 4,880

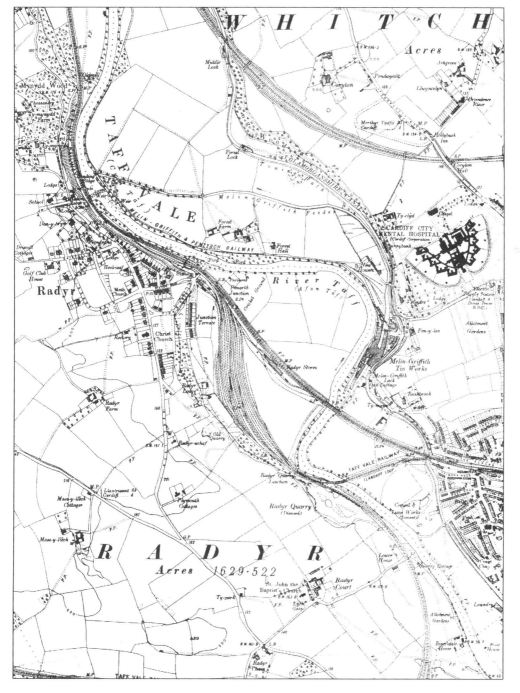

The parish of Radyr lies to the east of the River Taff on this map of 1922. St John's Church and Radyr Court are now both in the electoral district of Llandaff.

St John's has been the parish church of Radyr for at least 800 years but its appearance today is largely the result of a major restoration in the 19th century.

While the remains of an Iron Age cooking hearth in Radyr Wood indicate an earlier habitation, the first historical reference to Radyr comes in the 11th century, when a biographer of St Cadoc refers to 'the hamlet of Aradur between Llandaff and the forest'. It appears that a small hospice or hermitage at this site was sometimes visited by those making a pilgrimage to the shrine of Teilo at Llandaff.

The only two buildings of importance in the 13th century were St John's Church and the manor house at Radyr Court. St John's, which was built by Richard de Clare, retains some of its original features in the present structure, notably the chancel arch with its corbels originally intended to hold the rood beam. Hugh Despenser, the favourite of Edward II, was the owner of the manor in 1321, when the Mortimer family, bitter enemies of Hugh and the King, launched a devastating attack in which buildings were gutted, crops were destroyed and animals driven off.

In the 15th century Thomas Mathew acquired the manor of Radyr by marriage. He also enhanced his fortune through his position as Receiver of Ogmore and, after his death in 1470, his descendants carried on the family tradition of profitable matrimony. To reflect their riches, the old manor house on the west side of St John's was replaced with a fine two-storey building on a new site to the east of the church.

The family's wealth and influence in Radyr reached its peak under Sir George Mathew, who not only lived ostentatiously at Radyr Court, but also held the manor of Llandaff. He married twice and sired 24 children. His son, William, succeeded him in 1558 and he too had a large family. Ironically, their sexual prowess contributed to the family's decline as between them they fathered 21 daughters, all of whom were in need of dowries.

This drain on the estate was compounded by extravagance. Sir George built an impressive deer park at Radyr Court in 1536 but his son replaced it with an even more expensive one 60 years later. While a deer park was a mark of prestige to the Tudor gentry, its creation ensured that there was no income from the tenants that had previously occupied the land. Radyr Wood, at the rear of the High School and Woodfield Avenue, is now part of the former deer park.

By 1607 Edmund Mathew owed debts of £25,000. Among his creditors was his nephew, Sir Henry Billingsley, who issued a writ for the seizure of Radyr Court. Edmund resisted with armed force and the Sheriff withdrew, arguing that the house 'is not to be won without ordnance to batter it and shedding of much blood'. Remarkably Edmund's son, George, held on to Radyr Court for a few more years but in 1625 he sold it to Lewis of the Van and the Mathew interest in Radyr came to an end.

The Plymouth Estate owned most of Radyr by the end of the 18th century and its policy was to favour large, efficient farms. In 1836 Evan David of Radyr Court was farming 700 acres in Radyr, Llandaff and Fairwater. The old manor house had been largely demolished and the surviving part turned into a farmhouse.

For most of the 19th century Radyr was little more than a hamlet of scattered cottages, relying on agriculture as the basis of its economy. In 1851 its population was only 417 but changes were beginning to take place. As the ironworks at Pentyrch increased its labour force, new housing was needed for the workers. In 1841 there were 10 cottages at Pentre Poeth, the 'village of fire', and the number grew steadily until 1878. While there is some doubt about how Pentre Poeth became known as Morganstown, it was probably named after Morgan Williams who leased his land for the early development of the district.

Radyr Court in 1955. When the Danescourt Estate was built, the future of this historic building was in doubt but its conversion to a public house saved it from destruction.

Morganstown has grown considerably since these cottages were built along Ty-Nant Road over 100 years ago.

The arrival of the railway in 1859 heralded the emergence of fresh commercial activity in Radyr. Penarth Junction proved to be a convenient marshalling yard for the Taff Vale and Penarth Dock Railways, as an ever increasing volume of coal was transported from the mining valleys to the docks at Penarth and Cardiff. The sidings lay to the east of Radyr Wood and, at the same time, another siding was built for the use of the local quarry. Radyr stone had been used on a small scale for centuries but it was not until the 1850s that large-scale commercial exploitation began, when the quarry to the south of Radyr Station was opened. It provided major employment for the next 60 years as the stone was used for building work in and around Cardiff.

When a passenger station was built in 1883, professional people began to seek homes in the peaceful surroundings of Radyr, while still having easy access to their offices in Cardiff. By 1901 fine houses had been built along Heol Isaf and Station Road. Among them were Dan-y-Bryn, now the Cheshire Home, and Bryn Teg, the residence of Radyr's first doctor, which later became the Radyr Arms. St John's Church was restored in 1869 and Christchurch in Heol Isaf, a splendid example of neo-Gothic architecture, was built in 1910. New chapels, a school and shops provided for the differing needs of a growing population. The cricket club, established in 1890, and a beautiful golf course, opened in 1902, added to the appeal of Radyr as a desirable place to live.

Christchurch stands out in this view of Heol Isaf, the main road through Radyr. The photograph was taken before World War One.

In the 1930s Radyr was still very much a village community, as this peaceful scene above Heol Isaf indicates.

Roald Dahl referred to Ty-Mynydd as, 'a mighty house with turrets on its roof and with majestic lawns and terraces all around it'. This photograph was taken in World War Two, when Ty-Mynydd was used as the Docks Office.

The splendid 18th-century farmhouse at Ty Mynydd was transformed into a Gothic mansion by George Fisher, deputy chairman of the Taff Vale Railway. In 1918 Harald and Sofie Dahl with their six children, including Roald aged two, moved to Ty Mynydd with its acres of farmland and a very large staff. The family only lived there for two years, as Harald Dahl died in 1920 and Sofie moved to Llandaff. The house was demolished in 1967 after vandals started a fire in the empty building.

Until World War Two, Radyr continued to grow steadily but in the 1960s an extensive housing programme began to the west of Heol Isaf. Later the Danescourt Estate, though it lies within the electoral division of Llandaff, was built on land surrounding Radyr Court. Under the nearby shopping centre and the garden of Radyr Court, which is now a public house, lie the foundations of the old manor. Radyr became a suburb of Cardiff in 1974 and, despite the urbanisation of the last 40 years, which is still continuing with a new housing development at Radyr Farm, it remains one of Cardiff's most attractive suburbs.

Further Reading:

Radyr & Morganstown New Horizons History Group, *Twixt Chain and Gorge*, Radyr & Morganstown New Horizons Group, 1991

Radyr & Morganstown New Horizons History Group, *Memories of Radyr and Morganstown*, Radyr & Morganstown New Horizons Group, 1993

RHIWBINA

Population: 11,210

A small, ancient earthwork, near the summit of the Wenallt, suggests that there was a settlement at Rhiwbina in the Iron Age. Roman relics, found on Rhiwbina Hill, indicate that they too may have had a camp, where it would command a wide view of the surrounding area

The Twmpath is another site that has fascinated historians and archaeologists for many years. This mound, standing on a ridge 300 feet below the Wenallt, was thought by some to be the burial place of a Welsh chief, possibly Iestyn ap Gwrgant. A legend records that he fought a mighty battle against the Norman invaders near Nant Waedlyd, which means in English 'the Bloody Brook'. The tale goes on to say that Iestyn was killed and buried with his wealth under this mound. A wizard then cursed anyone who disturbed the site, saying: 'The first to put sword, spear or spade into this earth will be struck by lightning'. About 150 years ago some adventurous souls started digging in the hope of finding buried treasure. Thunder and lightning burst forth and the men fled in terror. Since then the site has beeen thoroughly excavated but nothing has been found. Probably the Twmpath was a Norman motte, acting as a small fort and observation point.

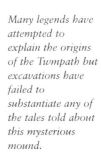

Many legends have attempted to explain the origins of the Twmpath but excavations have failed to substantiate any of the tales told about this mysterious mound.

In this view of the Deri, c.1928, the old oak can be seen to the left of the café which is now a general store.

The garden village in the 1920s. At its heart is Y-Groes, built around the green in the centre. At the foot of the photograph, Pen-y-Dre and Beulah Road meet at Heol-y-Deri, as it runs northwards towards what was then open countryside.

Before World War One, Rhiwbina was sparsely populated. Greenhill, the home of the Booker family, was a fine mansion and a few houses were scattered along Beulah Road, named after Beulah Congregational Chapel. Near the Masons' Arms and Tyn-y-Parc Farm were a cluster of small cottages and two small flannel factories.

There were a number of large farms, such as the Deri, Pantmawr, Tyn-y-Cae, Pen-y-Groes and Tyn-y-Coed, all familiar placenames in Rhiwbina today. For many years Rhiwbina Farm was owned by the Morgan family, who were related to Lord Tredegar. The farm has gone and the reservoir, built by the Cardiff Corporation in 1884 to supplement the needs of a growing borough, is now covered over.

The Deri is named after an oak tree which, despite being blasted by lightning, is still standing today. The fertile soil of Rhiwbina lent itself to arable farming and the Deri Mill was used to grind corn. The landlord of the nearby Butcher's Arms applied for his wine and spirit licence in 1861 on the basis that the mill was very busy and farmers travelling long distances needed sustenance. He added that visitors to Beulah Chapel for special services also needed liquid refreshment.

RHUBINA FIELDS
CARDIFF WORKER'S CO-OPERATIVE
GARDEN VILLAGE SOCIETY
LIMITED.

"Health for the Child"

Rail from Rhymney Station
Motor Bus from North Road.

This advertisement with its slogan, 'Health for the child', expresses the ideals of the Rhiwbina Garden Village Society.

In 1911 Professor Stanley Jevons resigned his position as Chair of Economics at University College in Cardiff to found the Housing Reform Company. He visualised a series of well-planned, beautiful garden suburbs around Cardiff and early in 1912 the first society was registered. It became the Rhiwbina Garden Village Society and was run on co-operative lines.

The houses were intended for 'skilled artisans, clerks, shop assistants and others of moderate incomes'. Each resident held shares and had a voice in the running of the society. The ultimate aim was a large suburb but initially 10 acres were purchased from the Pentwyn Estate near Rhiwbina Halt. A plaque, unveiled by the Earl of Plymouth, commemorates the completion of the first 34 houses in Lon Isa, Y-Groes and Lon-y-Dail in 1913.

The Housing Reform Company was wound up in World War One but, after hostilities had ceased, the Welsh Town Planning and Housing Trust covered liabilities and made funds available to build another 270 dwellings. In the end, only 189 were built, as many people preferred buying rather than renting their homes. The Depression also slowed progress in the early 1930s.

A solitary van enters Lon-y-Dail from Pen-y-Dre in 1926. Beulah Chapel is facing us in the centre of the photograph.

The houses built by the society were spaced at no more than 10 to an acre and varied in appearance. Some were semi-detached and others were in clusters of three or four. All houses from the outset had a bath, running water, electric light and a pleasant garden that tenants were expected to keep tidy. The society had rules which may have appeared fussy to some but which were drawn up democratically and maintained standards. One of the benefits offered by the society was the employment of a maintenance staff, thus avoiding any shoddy workmanship.

Shops, churches and a library were built to meet the needs of the growing village and a recreation club was opened in 1922. Six years later, Rhiwbina School was built and at that time it was the largest elementary school in Glamorgan. Opposite the school is the Memorial Hall, which was opened by Lady Mountbatten in 1957 as a tribute to the fallen of two world wars.

Inevitably, other property developers decided to build houses in Rhiwbina and this trend gained fresh impetus in the 1960s, when Llanishen Fach Farm was sold to pave the way for a large estate. Not surprisingly Rhiwbina is a very popular place in which to live. Notable residents include Jack Jones, author of *River out of Eden* and *Off to Philadelphia in the Morning,* and Iorwerth Peate, founder of the Museum of Welsh Life at St Fagans. The countryside is not far away and one of the great attractions, not just for local people but for others as well, is a ramble or picnic at the summit of the Wenallt. This tract of beautiful woodland and heath has been carefully preserved in its natural state with magnificent views over Cardiff and the Bristol Channel.

In 1962 the people of Rhiwbina celebrated the 50th anniversary of the garden city project in style, but six years later, the decision was taken to offer tenant-shareholders the leases on their properties at favourable terms. The original concept had run its course and in 1976 the Rhiwbina Garden City Society was dissolved with its surplus funds given to charity. The urban growth of Rhiwbina has been better planned than most other suburbs and much of the credit for this must go to those pioneers who showed such vision in 1912. When Rhiwbina became a suburb of Cardiff in 1974, their far-sightedness was recognised, as soon afterwards the area west of Lon-y-Deri was designated a conservation area.

This splendid view of Rhiwbina from the Wenallt was taken in 1962 before the reservoir was covered.

Further Reading:
Chappell, E.L. *Old Whitchurch,* Merton Priory Press, 1994
Davies, W. *Rhiwbina Garden Village* D. Brown & Son, 1985

RIVERSIDE

Population: 13,170

*Riverside, 1922.
Wellington Street
has since been
widened and much
of its surrounding
area redeveloped.
However,
Pontcanna is still
unspoilt parkland
and the Recreation
Ground is now the
home of
Glamorgan cricket.*

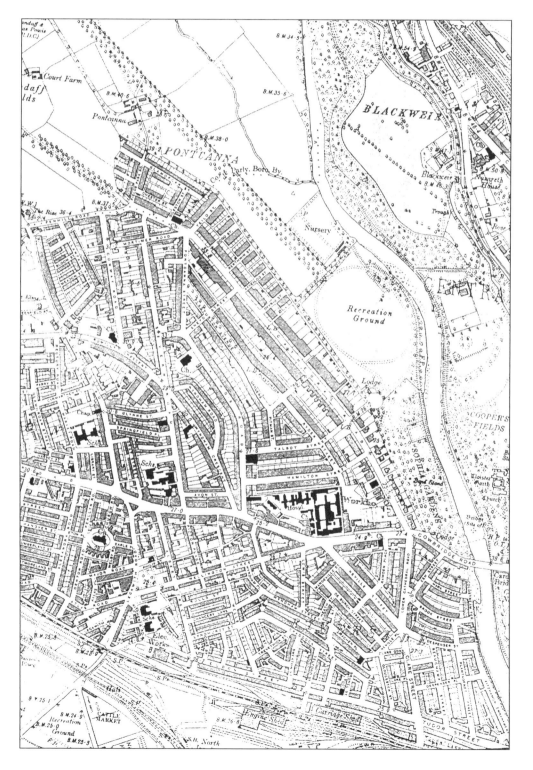

Riverside has been a suburb of Cardiff since 1875 and lies west of the River Taff from Tudor Road in the south to Western Avenue in the north. Old prints show sightseers looking across the river from Riverside towards Cardiff but few people settled in the district until the mid-19th century. The tithe map of 1841 shows a few cottages near Plas Turton, an old farm house which was demolished in 1895 to make way for Plasturton Avenue. Until 1858 access to Riverside and Canton from Cardiff was made through a toll gate, erected at the junction of Cowbridge Road and the lane that later became Cathedral Road.

Cowbridge Road in 1910. The Workhouse is on the left and it was in a house opposite here that Ivor Novello was born.

The first important public building in Riverside was the Union Workhouse in Cowbridge Road. Opened in 1836, it was a place where only the desperate sought refuge. To obtain parish relief, the whole family had to enter the workhouse. Men were sent to one ward, wives and children to another, and their meetings were restricted to 45 minutes a day. The regime was monotonous and hard. Men chopped wood, broke stones or carried coal, while the women worked in the laundry, helped to clean the building, or picked oakum. By 1900 the regime was less harsh. Many families were able to avoid the workhouse regime, as the authorities granted them a few shillings a week in outdoor relief, the forerunner of the retirement pension and unemployment benefit. Within the workhouse, trusted inmates were allowed out so long as they returned by 7pm, thereby avoiding the temptation of alcohol. In time the workhouse became a hospital, changing its name first to the City Lodge and then St David's Hospital. The site has now been redeveloped to provide a smaller hospital and housing accommodation, though the façade of the old building remains.

Sophia Gardens, laid out on land provided by the Marchioness of Bute and named after her, was opened in 1857. The *Cardiff and Merthyr Guardian* described it as, 'an ornamental walk and pleasure ground of exquisite taste in design which, for its extent and magnificence, will be unparalleled by anything of the sort in Wales'. The Marchioness only visited the park once but she did pay for a handsome fountain to be erected in the lake at the northern end of the park. The lake has gone and the character of Sophia Gardens has changed through the years. After World War Two, the Sophia Gardens Pavilion was erected and used for dances, public meetings and exhibitions. The boxing programme was also held in this former aeroplane hangar during the Empire Games of 1958. The pavilion came to a spectacular end when it collapsed under a heavy fall of snow in 1982. Much of Sophia Gardens today is occupied by Glamorgan Cricket Club and the Welsh Sports Centre. The cricket ground has splendid facilities and a number of one-day international matches have been played there in recent years.

By 1870 a cluster of houses had grown up around Mark Street, Green Street and Brook Street. Further west, working-class accommodation had been built in the area around Wellington Street, where the Salvation Army later founded a citadel. These Christian souls never wearied of trying to convert the ungodly, even when they were pelted with rubbish in the poorer streets of Canton and Riverside. In the 1970s, the 19th-century dwellings were replaced with modern housing and Wellington Street was widened.

There is a contrasting mixture of Victorian and Edwardian dwellings in the suburb. By the end of the 20th century, many homes in the area around Ninian Park

Sophia Gardens in the early 20th century. The trees are still attractive but a substantial part of the grounds, where the children are playing, is now required for car parking.

Development in Riverside is well under way in this photograph of 1870 but there are still open spaces on both sides of Cowbridge Road as it leads to Canton.

Llandaff Fields in the early 20th century before Western Avenue was built. The tree on the left is gone but the fountain, a gift from Mrs. H.M. Thompson in 1900, remains.

Road were showing signs of deterioration. A report of 1990 considered South Riverside to be 'the worst place to live in Cardiff', with 579 houses unfit to live in and over 1,000 in a serious state of disrepair. A 10-year plan costing £50 million was launched in 1993 in an attempt to remedy matters. Just south of Cowbridge Road, better-quality homes were built in the vicinity of Neville Street, De Burgh Street, Clare Street and Despenser Street. All these roads took their names from the mediaeval lords of Glamorgan.

In 1898, aided by a gift of £5,000 from Charles and Herbert Thompson, the council purchased Llandaff fields from the ecclesiastical commissioners. Herbert Thompson requested 'that the fields will be kept as fields, and that no attempt will be made to turn them into a park. Lavish expenditure would probably do little or nothing to improve the natural beauty they at present possess'. As a result of such foresight and later gifts from the Bute family, Riverside has nearly two miles of open countryside, bordering the river from Sophia Gardens to Western Avenue.

This beautiful environment encouraged developers to build splendid houses in Cathedral Road and the surrounding district of Pontcanna. Most of these fine buildings are now used as consulting rooms or offices. They include the former Cardiff United Synagogue which was opened in 1897 to serve the Jewish community, many of whom lived in this part of Cardiff at that time.

Number 11 Cathedral Road is named 'Novello House' after the famous actor, composer and West End producer, Ivor Novello. He was born in 1893 a short distance away in Cowbridge Road, where a plaque reads:

'This boy became a Ruritanian King

Who gave his people dreams and songs to sing'.

Cathedral Road before World War One. The street is still one of the finest Victorian thoroughfares in Britain, despite some ugly modern buildings near Cowbridge Road.

Later the family moved to Cathedral Road and then to London. Soon after the outbreak of World War One, Ivor wrote one of the greatest songs from that conflict, *Keep the Home Fires Burning*. From 1934 until his death in 1951, Ivor's talent reached its full flowering with a Novello musical invariably playing somewhere in the West End.

Flooding has been a problem for the people of Riverside whenever the Taff bursts its banks. The council attempted to solve the problem in 1849, when the course of the river was altered, but serious floods continued to occur until the late 20th century. The last deluge ocurred in 1979, following which new measures were taken which have so far proved successful. However, some residents are apprehensive that the barrage at Cardiff Bay might cause future problems with a rise in the level of groundwater.

It was on 2 January 1941 that Riverside experienced the most traumatic night in its history. The air raid siren sounded at 6.40pm and in the next few hours terror rained down on Cardiff, especially in Riverside. Landmines cut a swathe of devastation through Neville Street and the surrounding area. Blackstone Street was completely destroyed and seven people, who earlier that day had attended a funeral, were killed by a direct hit on the house where they were taking shelter. Riverside has changed little since the war but, when you walk around De Burgh Place or Neville Street, you can see post-war houses rebuilt in red brick, standing among the pennant sandstone homes of an earlier, more peaceful age.

Further Reading

Jones, B. *Canton*, Chalford Press, 1995

The ruins of the Conservative Club in De Burgh Place after the raid of 2 January 1941. In the first hour of the attack, 60 people were killed in Riverside.

RUMNEY

Population: 8,970

Rumney in 1922 was still a rural parish in Monmouthshire. The Rumney Pottery, St Augustine's Church and the Carpenter's Arms remain as a testimony to the past, but the farms have given way to an urban suburb.

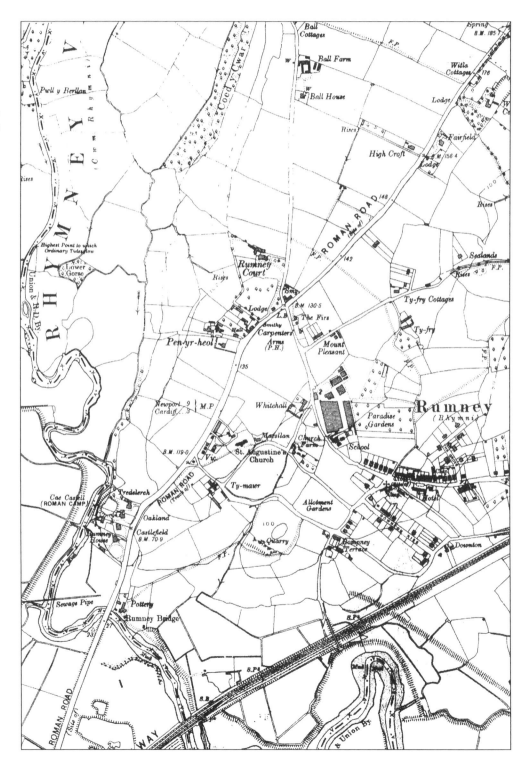

The Welsh name for Rumney is 'Tredelerch', supposedly referring to a time when swans were found in great numbers near the River Rhymney. Roman pottery has been found on the foreshore near Newton Farm while Caer Castell, where Rumney High School and St Illtyd's College are now sited, was probably a Roman fortification. Another local placename, 'Lamby', has a Scandinavian origin, suggesting that the Danes may have traded along the river.

St Augustine's, a place of worship for over 800 years, was still a country church when this photograph was taken in 1908.

Where Castle Heights now stands, the Normans built a motte and bailey castle and soon afterwards the manor of Rompney became established as a part of the mediaeval comitatus of Wentloog. Its owners have included Gilbert de Clare, Edmund, the Earl of Stafford and Thomas Cromwell, who received the estate as a gift from Henry VIII in 1532. He only held the manor for a short time, as he became a victim of Henry's unreliable temper and was executed as a traitor. The manor later became a farm which ceased to exist when Ty Mawr Road and Ty Mawr Avenue were built in the 1930s. The manor house itself was situated at the junction of these two roads. The lord's two water mills, which were constantly being repaired in the Middle Ages, have also disappeared. They may have been a prime target for Welsh raiders who caused widespread destruction in 1294 and 1316.

It was the responsibility of the lord's tenants to maintain the sea wall and collect earth to support its gowts or stone gates. These gowts prevented the sea from flooding at high tide, while allowing surplus fresh water to disperse into the sea. When the feudal system came to an end, this duty was undertaken by the parish.

The Rompney Arms, formerly the Pear Tree, in Wentloog Road. Its present style dates from its renovation in 1932.

Rumney Bridge and pottery, c.1914. The river was the boundary between Glamorgan and Monmouthshire until Rumney became a suburb of Cardiff.

The 12th-century church of St Augustine, with its vicarage and 40 acres of land, was awarded to the Abbey of Bristol by William, Lord of Glamorgan. The original tower was rebuilt in the 15th century, though the doorway appears to be Norman. The mediaeval font still survives but perhaps the most interesting feature of the church is its six bells, the oldest dating back to 1709.

A stone stile from the churchyard leads to a row of cottages known as Beili Bach, or the little bailey. Beili Bach is at least 300 years old and was originally a thatched, single-storey farmhouse, where the family shared their accommodation with the animals. An additional storey was built later, using stone from the nearby quarry.

An Exchequer deposition of 1609 alleges that Rumney was the most unruly place in Monmouthshire. When Thomas Powell, an under-sheriff, tried to arrest a group of criminals, his life was in danger when they were forcibly rescued by neighbours. Nearly 200 years later, in 1793, the people of Rumney acted as peacemakers. A band of sailors, thought to be mutineers and armed with cutlasses and bludgeons, were pursued by the press gang as they set out from Cardiff towards Newport. A pitched battle was fought at Rumney, where the outnumbered press gang were rescued by local people who pacified the sailors with a pint of ale at the Pear Tree Inn.

This tavern was reputedly a favourite haunt for smugglers, though there are legends that they used Beili Bach to hide their contraband and also met at the manor house, where there was a secret passage down to the river. The Pear Tree was purchased in the 19th century by the first American Consul in Cardiff, who added

Newport Road was much narrower in the early 20th century, when the Carpenter's Arms was just one of the public houses in Rumney attracting visitors from Cardiff on Sundays.

Rumney Hill in the 1930s. These houses were to lose part of their front gardens when the road was widened in 1967.

a mock baronial hall and renamed it the Rompney Arms. Nowadays, it is a popular pub with an attractive Tudor-style façade.

A strong, one-arched bridge was built across the river when the Cardiff Turnpike Trust began the construction of a new road from Rumney Bridge to Bonvilston. Tolls were collected at a house which was demolished just before World War Two. This house stood next to the Rumney Pottery, one of the oldest buildings in the district. Owned by the Giles family since the early 19th century, high-quality products are still being manufactured at Rumney Pottery, as they have been for the last 300 years. At one time clay was imported but now it is taken from the banks along the river. The bottle-shaped chimney of the kiln collapsed in World War Two after a bomb fell nearby, though part of the kiln can still be seen inside the pottery.

William Booth, writing in his *Rambles around Rumney*, observed that in 1892 Rumney was a straggling village, with houses built in threes and fours along lanes that ended in ditches. A few years later he observed that the village was waking up, as 'the number of shops has doubled. There are now two'. In 1901 its population of 579 were mostly farmers. Some of them bred horses and cattle but the majority supplied Cardiff with flowers, vegetables and milk.

At that time, the Rompney Arms, the Cross Inn and the Carpenter's Arms had a powerful attraction for residents of Cardiff on a Sunday. As pubs in Wales were closed on the Sabbath, people crossed Rumney Bridge into Monmouthshire where the taverns were still open. A local resident made a tongue-in-cheek comment about 'the very powerful sermons preached at Rumney'. Crowds would flock into the

village from Cardiff just before church on Sunday evening and later return in an excited state, 'staggering all over the road. Could it be that the sober, religious Welsh go into England to avoid the Sunday Closing Act'?

In 1887 Rumney was included in the county of Glamorgan for administrative affairs, though the parish remained in Monmouthshire. When Rumney Bridge needed widening and strengthening in 1910, the cost was borne jointly by the Cardiff and Monmouthshire councils. These closer ties paved the way for Rumney to become a suburb of Cardiff, a fact which was formally approved in 1938. At that time nearly 800 houses, mostly semi-detached, had been built south of Rumney Hill from New Road to Claremont Avenue.

After World War Two, Rumney's remaining open spaces became part of a massive housing development which eventually spread into Llanrumney, Trowbridge and St Mellons. Large houses on Rumney Hill and along Newport Road were swallowed up by modern housing estates. One of these splendid villas was Witla Court, which was built for the Heywoods, a wealthy Cardiff shipping firm. Colonel H.J. Heywood was a devout Roman Catholic who built a private chapel for his fellow worshippers alongside the house. Witla Court was used as a land army hostel in World War Two and, in the late 1960s, the estate was developed for housing.

Despite modern developments, Rumney remains a suburb of interesting contrasts. Not far from Lamby Industrial Park lie dwellings which are centuries old. One of them is Oakmeadow Cottage, a house which was used as a magistrate's court and

Witla Court, c.1900, when the Heywood family lived there. The property is now owned by the Monkstone Restaurant.

The 16th-century Oakmeadow Cottage off New Road is now a picturesque little house which belies its sinister past.

bore the threatening title of 'Hangman's Cottage'. A legend maintains that it was haunted by condemned prisoners. The larder was a cell where these wretches were held and chained to an iron ring. For many years the room had an obnoxious smell which a medium attributed to the stench of fear and, when the larder was knocked down, the smell disappeared.

The farms and fields that once dotted the landscape of Rumney are gone but pleasant open spaces can still be found. Tredelerch Park, near a landfill site in Lamby Way, has a 10-acre lake and was recently opened with the aim of emphasising the ecology and wildlife of the area. Rumney Gardens, built on the site of a former cemetery, overlooks pleasant woodland at the rear and offers a welcome respite from the busy traffic on Newport Road. The Quarry, which once supplied stone for the older buildings of the district, has also been converted into a pleasure garden, serving as a reminder of how past and present blend in this interesting suburb.

Further Reading:
Bielski, A. *The Story of St Mellons*, Alun Books, 1985
North, G.A. *Rumney and the Wentlooge Level*, Chalford Publishing Company, 1997

ST FAGANS

Population: 760

St Fagans was probably inhabited in prehistoric times, as a number of axe-heads and a spear-head have been found in the Plymouth Woods. According to Geoffrey of Monmouth, Ffagan, after whom the village is named, and his companion, Dyfan, brought Christianity to Britain and 'purged away the paganism of well-nigh the whole island'. This high praise is based on a very dubious tale of the second century, though a church, dedicated to St Fagan, once stood in the grounds of the castle.

Peter le Sore came into the possession of St Fagans after the Norman Conquest and built a motte and bailey castle to control the crossing of the River Ely. The le Sores held the estate for over 200 years before it passed through marriage to the le Vele family from Gloucestershire. In 1475, again because of a matrimonial alliance, David Mathew of Radyr became lord of the manor. At that time the original castle was already crumbling. Nothing of it now remains, but one relic from those mediaeval days is the holy well of St Fagan, situated between the two lower fishponds in the Museum of Welsh Life. According to Richard Symonds, who visited the site with Charles I in 1645, people came to drink at the well as a cure for epilepsy and, 'after they have drank of it they relate their health ever since'.

St Fagans has not changed very much since this aerial view was taken in the 1930s. The castle, the church and the premises of the old school remain but the thatched cottages near the railway line have gone, and the village no longer has a station.

St Fagans Castle in 1920, when the Plymouth family were its owners. The present building dates from the 16th and 17th century, but an earlier castle was built on the site by the Normans.

Dr John Gibbon bought the manor in 1560 and began to build the castle which is now part of the museum. He sold the property, still only half built, to his brother-in-law, Nicholas Herbert, who lacked the funds to complete the work. His son William desperately needed money to join Raleigh's ill-fated expedition to South America in 1616 and accepted an offer for the estate from Sir Edward Lewis of the Van.

This family, which could trace its ancestry back to the lords of Senghenydd, was one of the most influential in Glamorgan. Different branches of the family acquired estates in the Taff and Rhymney valleys, Llanishen, Whitchurch, Radyr, Penmark and St Fagans. Their wealth was probably the reason Charles I met the gentlemen of Glamorgan at St Fagans in 1645 in the hope of reviving his flagging fortunes.

Usually St Fagans was a sleepy, agricultural community, similar to others in the Vale of Glamorgan, but on 8 May 1648 this tranquillity was brutally disturbed. The Civil War, apparently at an end two years earlier, flared up again as Charles I plotted to regain his power. A motley crew of disillusioned Roundheads, who had fought with Parliament earlier in the war, joined forces with diehard Royalists against Cromwell's Model Army. In South Wales the Royalists, led by Major-General Rowland Laugharne, planned to seize Cardiff Castle as the first stage in setting the West Country ablaze.

His army was 8,000 strong but many of them were no more than bewildered farmhands, armed with pikes and pitchforks. They assembled at St Nicholas but, on hearing that Cromwell was hastening to Wales, Laugharne marched on Cardiff.

When Colonel Thomas Horton forestalled him by mounting a heavy guard at Ely Bridge, Laugharne was forced to look for an alternative route through St Fagans. Monday 8 May was a raw, unpleasant morning when the armies clashed on farmland to the north of the castle. Despite superiority in numbers, the Royalists were no match for Horton's hardened, professional army. Within two hours, Laugharne's makeshift forces were put to flight, relentlessly pursued by Horton's cavalry. From St Fagans alone, 65 men were killed and the harvest that year was gathered in by their widows. The River Ely was said to have run red with blood and, though the battle is rarely mentioned in English history books, it was the greatest and most significant clash of the Civil War in Wales.

In May 1998, to commemorate the 350th anniversary of the Battle of St Fagans, the Sealed Knot Society re-enacted the event in the grounds of the Museum of Welsh Life.

The castle dominated the village of St Fagans, which at that time consisted of little more than the green, the church, the mill near the bridge, and a few cottages and farmhouses. The church was dedicated to St Mary and its history can be traced back to the 12th century. Improvements in the 14th century produced a nave and chancel which are superb examples of mediaeval work. A restoration was carried out in 1860 and one of the stained-glass windows from that period depicts the ministry of St Fagan.

In 1730 the property passed to Other Windsor, the 3rd Earl of Plymouth, following his marriage to Elizabeth Lewis. During the 18th century, the new owners were usually absentee landlords and this was a time of stagnation, both for the castle and for the village. The situation changed in 1852 when Robert Windsor-Clive, heir to the estate, chose to live at St Fagans with his new bride, Mary. He died seven years later but Lady Windsor continued to live at the castle, and in 1868–69 carried out an extensive restoration.

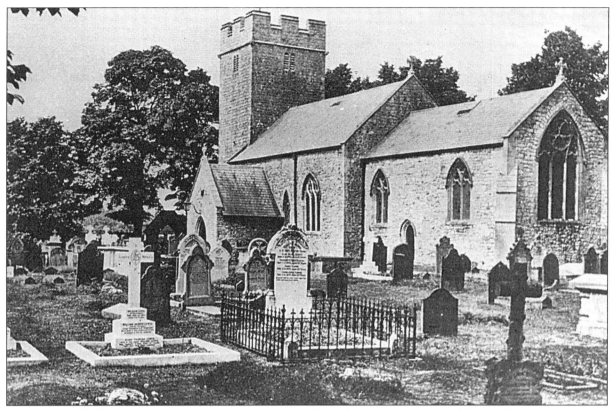

St Mary's Church, despite its Victorian restoration, retains clear evidence of its original Norman and Decorated styles of architecture.

These pretty thatched cottages on Castle Hill have scarcely changed since this picture was taken in 1936.

Considerable improvements were also made in the village, which one visitor described as 'one of the prettiest and cleanest little villages in the Vale'. St Fagans was virtually a model estate, where new homes were built for its workers, old cottages were refurbished and a national school was built in a Tudor style. By contrast, the Plymouth Arms was rebuilt in 1895 in a Jacobean style. To ensure that there was no unruly behaviour, a former butler from the castle was installed as landlord. He kept a strict regime, making it clear to customers that two pints of beer was their limit.

A paternal system existed until well into the 20th century. The parish was virtually self-sufficient, with one pub, one butcher, one shoemaker and one shop, one of each being sufficient for the village's needs. Most of the people in the village were employed on the estate. There was a great occasion in 1878 when Lady Mary's son came of age. A special train brought 400 of the family's Glamorgan tenants to St Fagans for a banquet at the castle, followed by a fireworks display and other entertainment. The festivities went on for two days, in which 300 chickens, four tons of meat and 25 hogsheads of ale were consumed. So much wine was drunk that extra supplies were required.

During the 20th century, the Plymouth family continued Lady Mary's paternal role at St Fagans, using the castle as a summer residence. More than 50 staff descended on the castle when it was used to entertain important visitors. Queen Mary stayed there in 1938 and a few years earlier the Prince of Wales had been among the guests. Before World War One, a banqueting hall for 40 people was built in the grounds which, during that war, became a military hospital.

The Plymouth Arms, 1908. Nowadays, it is both a pub and a popular restaurant which enjoys a thriving trade from the many visitors to St Fagans.

Between the two world wars, The Court was the home of Lord Glanely and later the Llewellyn family. The Court Nursing Home now occupies the site.

Another notable house in St Fagans, just off Michaelston Road, was The Court. This became the chosen residence of two families connected with the world of racing. When Lord Glanely, one of the foremost shipping magnates in Cardiff, lived there after World War One, his horses won every classic race including the Derby. After Glanely retired to Newmarket, the Llewellyn family lived at The Court. Harry Llewellyn was a keen horseman and finished second in the Grand National of 1936. His greatest moment came in 1952, when he was the captain of the equestrian team that won Britain's only gold medal in the Olympic Games in Helsinki.

In 1947 the Earl of Plymouth and his mother donated St Fagans Castle and its grounds to the National Museum of Wales as a site for a folk museum. Since that time, the Museum of Welsh Life has become one of the top tourist sites in the country, as buildings of all kinds have been acquired from every part of Wales.

The River Ely and the Plymouth Woods indicate why St Fagans, though a suburb of Cardiff, retains its rural past.

Among those rebuilt in the grounds are old farmhouses, miners' cottages, a chapel, a miners' institute, a postwar 'prefab' and even the 'house of the future'. Visitors can see craftsmen, such as the cooper or the blacksmith, practise their traditional crafts in an authentic setting. There are also three indoor museums and the castle itself, overlooking lovely gardens and parkland, is a great attraction.

The Museum of Welsh Life attracts nearly 700,000 visitors every year. The Gwalia Stores is just one example of the many restored buildings they come to see in a beautiful environment.

When the Earl of Plymouth made a gift of 45 acres of woodland between the new Ely housing estate and the river in 1922, it became a popular place for picnics and ramblers. Sadly, the Plymouth Woods have gained notoriety for crime and vandalism in recent years. St Fagans itself has remained a charming village since becoming a part of Cardiff in 1974. Housing development has been restricted to the areas around St Fagans Drive and The Court and, in terms of population, the suburb is the smallest in Cardiff. There are few more delightful ways of spending a summer's afternoon than to watch a game of cricket at the picturesque ground of the local club, the home of a team which a few years ago won the National Village Cricket Final at Lords.

Further Reading:

William, E. *St Fagans Castle and its Inhabitants,* National Museum of Wales, 1988
Shepherd, C.F. *The Parish of St Fagans* in Glamorgan Historian Vol. VIII p.75-88, Stewart Williams, 1974
Tilney, C. *The Battle of St Fagans* in Glamorgan Historian Vol. VIII p.89-104, Stewart Williams, 1974

Splott and Tremorfa

Population: 12,550

Since this map of Splott was compiled in 1922, the East Moors Works and the streets between Portmanmoor Road and the railway line have been replaced with new industries. Splott Park and Tremorfa lie east of the railway line.

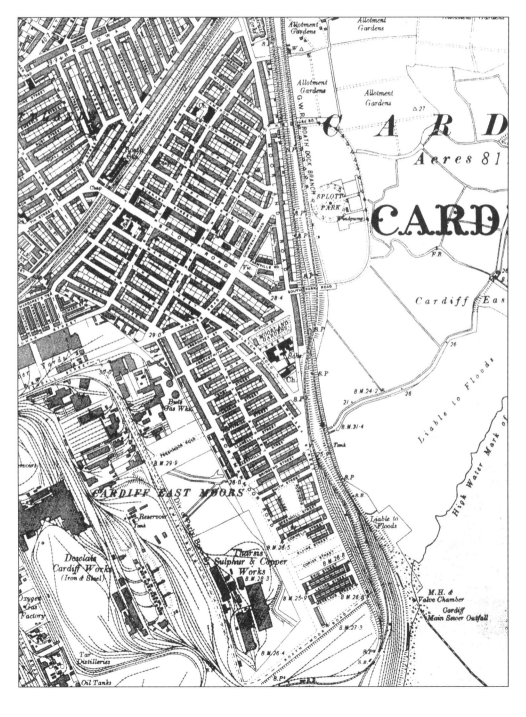

Prior to the Norman Conquest, Splott was an episcopal estate owned by the Bishop of Llandaff. Its unusual name has often aroused curiosity and is possibly an abbreviated term for 'God's Plot'. For centuries, the manor of Splott was little more than open moorland, which was acquired by Thomas Bawdripp of Penmark in the 16th century. It was later sold to Edward Lewis of the Van before eventually becoming a part of the Tredegar Estate in 1676.

A map of Splott and Tremorfa in 1789 shows little else but the three farms of Pengam and Upper and Lower Splott. The Splott farms were worked as one unit and in 1840 covered 378 acres, most of it moorland. This remained the situation until Cardiff began its rapid growth in the 19th century. By 1891 several industrial and commercial enterprises were established at East Moors and, during that year, the opening of the Dowlais Steelworks transformed the area.

The company had begun its existence in Merthyr but, as it became necessary to import iron ore from abroad, its production costs rose considerably. A decision was taken to build a modern furnace at East Moors on land owned by Lord Bute, who performed the opening ceremony on 4 February 1891. Amalgamations with other steel makers before World War One created the industrial giant of Guest, Keen and Nettlefolds with a capital of £3 million. The parent company at Merthyr was now dwarfed by its offspring and in 1934 a further investment resulted in a large integrated plant, capable of manufacturing half a million tons of steel a year. For

In 1927 the Dowlais Works was the most important industrial employer in Cardiff. There was a price for local residents to pay as their homes became coated with a fine red dust from the furnace.

Splott Park, 1911. The bandstand was erected six years earlier and entertainment was usually provided by the Splott Temperance Band.

nearly 90 years the great furnaces and chimney stacks of the East Moors Works, casting their red glow at night, were a familiar part of the skyline in Splott and Tremorfa.

At first the building of houses in Splott proceeded slowly and a street directory for 1891 shows most of them clustered around Sanquar Street, Splott Road and Habershon Street. To provide homes for the thousands of workers employed by the new steel works, the pace of building accelerated towards Portmanmoor Road and Moorland Road. By World War One, the rail link to Roath Dock was the dividing line between a built-up Splott to the west and the open fields of Tremorfa to the east.

Lord Tredegar presented Splott Park to the Corporation in 1901 and it was soon one of the best equipped in Cardiff. It had cricket pitches and nets, when these were a rarity on public parks, a bowling green and a bandstand. The park also provided playing facilities for local clubs and schools.

The earliest school to be built in the area was Splottlands, which had 1,500 pupils when it opened in 1882. Since its demolition in 1971, the Star Sports and Recreation Centre has occupied the site. Moorland Road School became renowned for its sporting reputation and can count Welsh football internationals Billy James and Ron Stitfall among its scholars. Shirley Bassey also went to school at Moorland Road when, at the age of two, her family moved to Portmanmoor Road. The Splott University Settlement, established in Courtenay Road with the aim of promoting education and recreation among the poor, was famous for its baseball team, which

Right: E.T. Willows was a pioneer aviator who was fascinated with airships. Unfortunately, though possessing a creative mind, he was never able to turn his ideas into financial success.

drew crowds of up to 20,000. In 1924 the premises were acquired by St Illtyd's College, the first Catholic grammar school in Wales.

Ernest Willows once said: 'As a boy I remember jumping off a bank with an open umbrella in my hand, just to make believe I was flying'. His love of flying led to experiments with airships in a large shed, built on the open spaces of East Moors. Willows successfully manoeuvred his first invention 120 feet above the ground on 5 September 1905 and, five years later, he won a prize of £50 when he became the first man to fly over Cardiff. He navigated his craft from East Moors to the City Hall, landing near the statue of Lord Tredegar. Further adventures followed but the airships developed by Willows were never commercially viable. He failed to see that the future lay with fixed-wing aircraft and he suffered a succession of business failures. In 1926 he was tragically killed when the basket broke away from the balloon in which he was flying. However, it is a fitting tribute to Willows's spirit of adventure that the school, later built on land where he began his experiments, bears his name.

Though Pengam ceased to be a working farm in 1936, a major housing programme in Tremorfa was delayed until after World War Two. In 1930 Cardiff's new municipal airport was opened on Pengam Moors near the farm. An early visitor was the Prince of Wales, who arrived at the airport wearing a flying helmet and goggles. Later that day he opened the Chemistry and Physics Laboratory at University College. In the 1930s the Great Western Railway offered domestic flights to Torquay at a single fare of £3 and by 1938 there was a regular service to Weston

Pengam Farm, 1930. The recently opened municipal airport was nearby and the onlookers at the roadside are probably taking an interest in its activities.

every hour. The 10-minute journey cost 9s 6d for a return ticket. The airport was an RAF maintenance unit during the war and its principal role was to act as a packing depot for aircraft destined for overseas service. Its short runway, lack of night flying facilities and proximity to residential areas led to the closure of Cardiff Municipal Airport in 1954 but many of its former hangars in Seawall Road are still used as workshops and factories.

After World War Two, Cardiff found difficulty in retaining its manufacturing industries, many of which were based in Splott and Tremorfa. The Rover Car Company set up a factory at Tremorfa in 1963 but only an eighth of the anticipated jobs materialised, and these were lost when the works closed in the 1980s. Even more disastrous was the loss of 3,000 jobs at the East Moors Steelworks. By 1978 its equipment had become obsolete and, with annual losses of £15 million, the decision was taken to close the plant.

These were body blows to Splott and Tremorfa, where many of these workers lived, but in recent years an attempt has been made to rejuvenate the district. Houses in and around Portmanmoor Road were demolished in the 1970s and replaced with an industrial estate. Similar estates and a business park were later built on land once occupied by the steelworks. If the necessary finance can be found, a proposal to construct the East Bay Road, hugging the foreshore of Splott and Tremorfa, would give access to a large area of land capable of further development.

Further Reading:

Childs, J. *Roath, Splott and Adamsdown,* Chalford Publishing Company, 1995

Aeroplanes of Cambrian Air Services at Pengam Airport in 1953. A year later, civil flights were transferred to Rhoose and the airport's 24-year history drew to a close.

TROWBRIDGE AND NEW ST MELLONS

Population: 17,530

The Trowbridge electoral division, which includes the southern part of St Mellons, is one of Cardiff's newer suburbs. Less than 40 years ago it was a rural area of low-lying land, across which ran the main railway line to Bristol. It was thinly populated apart from a few farms and its history, with one exception, had been largely uneventful.

The exception was the worst natural disaster ever to strike South Wales. On 20 January 1607 tempestuous winds in the Bristol Channel created a flood similar to a tidal wave. An unknown chronicler recorded the disaster in a broadsheet entitled *Woeful Newes From Wales*. He wrote that the waters, four miles wide, swept across the region, 'with a swiftness so incredible … that no greyhound could have escaped by running before them'. Houses were destroyed, cattle perished and wild animals, in their fear, no longer preyed on each other. The death toll was estimated at 2,000 as the sea defences, both on the English and the Welsh sides, were submerged. In Monmouthshire alone, 26 parishes were 'drowned' and five years were to pass before the soil recovered from its contamination by the sea.

Amid this turmoil, there were some miraculous escapes. A baby was discovered bobbing about on the waters in a cradle which a cat was able to balance by jumping

Looking towards Trowbridge from the sea in 2002. In the past this low-lying land suffered serious flooding from time to time.

from side to side. In another house, a little girl was found snuggling up to a chicken in the beams of the roof, where her mother had hastily placed her. Climbing trees did not always save people but one couple, 'espying nothing but death before them', were saved when an empty tub gave them a lifeline as it floated against a tree.

The whole of Cardiff was flooded but it was the parishes on low-lying land east of the borough that suffered most. At Peterstone Wentloog to the east of St Mellons, a memorial plaque on the outside of the church, using the old style of dating, commemorates 'The Great Flood, January 20th, 1606'. There were to be no more catastrophes on this scale, though flooding continued to be a problem for many years.

In the 1960s the land now comprising Trowbridge and New St Mellons was prepared for domestic and industrial development. In 1964 the post-war housing estate in Rumney was extended to the east, swallowing up the farms of Trowbridge Fawr (Greater Trowbridge) and Trowbridge Bach (Little Trowbridge). As the demand for new homes increased, St Mellons was brought into the city's boundaries in 1974 and the southern part of this parish provided the land for another large housing programme.

Other areas in the district were allocated to accommodate units of light industry and commerce. The Spring Meadow Business Park, the Wentloog Industrial Park and the Freight Liner Depot are all based on former farmland in Trowbridge. The St Mellons and the Links business parks are set in a pleasant tree-lined environment not far from St Mellons Golf Course.

This unknown artist's portrayal of the Great Flood shows the desperation of people trying to escape its terrible surge. The spire of Peterstone Church is an indication of the depth of the waters.

The St Mellons Business Park is one of a number of new commercial developments which provide a pleasant working environment in this suburb of Cardiff.

However, both the Trowbridge and the St Mellons estates have had their difficulties. In Trowbridge particularly, matters have not been helped by the dreary appearance of the shopping centre and some of the early houses, typical of the architecture of the 1960s. The quality of housing on the New St Mellons Estate is better and, at Melrose Park and Cypress Drive, there are some very attractive dwellings. In 1998 local people claimed they were 'the forgotten Cardiff estate' and a social services report designated the area as the second most deprived in Wales. There were complaints from residents of vandalism, crime, graffiti, litter and a lack of facilities, especially for youngsters. One person with enough talent to overcome these problems was Craig Bellamy. He was brought up in Trowbridge and his skills as a footballer have led him to stardom with Newcastle United and Wales.

Efforts are being made to improve the environment of this suburb. Street lighting has improved and more CCTV cameras have been installed. Some of the worst buildings, including the shopping centre at Trowbridge, are being demolished and rebuilt. Pockets of anti-social behaviour remain but co-operation involving the council, the police and local residents' groups is encouraging people to take a greater pride in their area.

The poor reputation that Trowbridge is sometimes given is belied by this pleasant view at Trowbridge Green.

Further Reading:
Bielski, A. *The Story of St Mellons*, Alun Books, 1985
Anon *Woefull Newes from Wales*, British Museum, 1891

WHITCHURCH AND TONGWYNLAIS

Population: 15,400

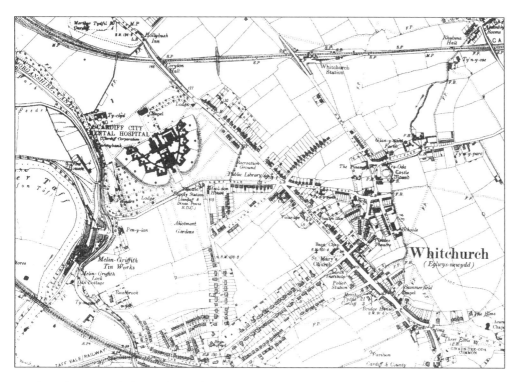

Whitchurch in 1922 was a village surrounded by open fields on which houses have since been built. Beyond the Hollybush Inn, the road continues towards Tongwynlais and Pontypridd, the principal route from Cardiff to the valleys at that time.

Little is known of the 'White Church' that gives Whitchurch its name and the first official reference to the district occurs in an agreement between Bishop Urban and Robert, Earl of Gloucester, in 1126. The Earl granted land and tithes in Whitchurch to Llandaff Cathedral and a chapel was built where Old Church Road now stands. It remained a dependency of the cathedral until 1845, when Whitchurch became a parish in its own right.

After the Norman Conquest, the Welsh were forced to yield the lowlands of Glamorgan to the invaders but, for 150 years in the hills north of Cardiff, the lords of Senghenydd stubbornly fought to retain their lands, their customs and their Welsh laws. In 1266 Gilbert de Clare finally mounted a successful campaign which resulted in the downfall of Gruffydd ap Rhys, last Lord of Senghenydd.

The invaders had prevailed and the manor of Whitchurch, comprising northern Whitchurch, Rhiwbina, Llandaff North and Melingriffith, was now created. The headquarters of the manor were situated in Old Church Road and it was protected

Castell Coch was originally a mediaeval defensive measure at Tongwynlais. Set in beautiful woodland above the village, its imaginative 19th-century restoration by William Burges has led to it being used in the making of several films.

by a stone tower which proved to be incapable of withstanding a serious attack. It is uncertain when it was destroyed but it was no longer in use by the 16th century. A grassy mound originally marked its site but this was removed when flats were built in 1966.

When Llywelyn ap Gruffydd destroyed the half-built fortifications at Caerphilly Castle in 1270, Gilbert de Clare decided to build Castell Coch, the 'Red Castle', both to protect the river crossing at Tongwynlais and the approach to Cardiff. It served its purpose at the time but the castle was a ruin by the 16th century. Evidence of mining activities and damage by fire suggest that it was attacked at some stage, possibly by Owain Glyndwr.

Following the Reformation, the lords of Cardiff, the first of whom was the Earl of Pembroke, inherited the manor of Whitchurch. While important local families, such as the Morgans of Tredegar, the Earls of Plymouth and the Lewises of the Van, possessed estates in Whitchurch at some time or other, no single landowner dominated the parish.

Until the mid-18th century, the population of the district was probably no more than 300 people, living in about 50 small farms and cottages. Tenants were free to graze their animals on Whitchurch Common and a fertile soil produced enough grain to justify the presence of the mills at Melingriffith, Little Mill and Tongwynlais. There were also several smithies, usually based at public houses such as the Plough, the Three Horseshoes and the Three Elms.

In 1749 the Melingriffith Mill became a source of power for the manufacturing of iron and tinplate. At the end of the 18th century, the Melingriffith Works was sending 13,000 boxes of tinplate a year to Bristol for distribution throughout the country. Soon afterwards the company benefited from the opening of the Glamorganshire Canal which flowed past the works and provided transport for its raw materials and finished products. The Melingriffith Tinplate Company continued to prosper under the direction of Richard Blakemore and his nephew, Thomas Booker. In 1870 the firm's 12 mills were producing 100,000 boxes of tinplate and 10,000 tons of sheet iron a year.

The Melingriffith Works in 1910. For more than a century, thousands of tons of tinplate were transported from the works along the Glamorganshire Canal.

Thereafter the works began to decline. Difficulties arose after the Franco-Prussian War when a slump in trade, a number of bad debts and failure to modernise led to bankruptcy. Initially, Melingriffith was saved by leasing it to the Cardiff Iron and Tinplate Company. In 1888 the company was purchased by Richard Thomas and remained in production, apart from a period in World War Two, until 1957.

Tongwynlais grew rapidly between 1840 and 1860 as workers at the Pentyrch and Melingriffith Works needed somewhere to live. It soon became as busy as Whitchurch and had its own weekly market. The village smithy was a place where people met for a gossip and, as the smith was also keeper of the pound for stray animals, the charges he collected were a lucrative source of income. The weighbridge near Tongwynlais Lock was always a busy place, where there were perhaps a dozen barges waiting at times. Serious congestion often led to loss of temper and sometimes fisticuffs. The annual Ton Fair in August was a popular occasion, when a funfair was set up amid stalls selling flannel and wool. The third day was always the Boatmen's Fair, a special holiday for canal workers.

One notable resident at Tongwynlais was Wyndham Lewis, who was MP for Cardiff until Lord Bute withdrew his patronage in 1826. Lewis then became MP for Maidstone and a colleague of Disraeli. He married Mary Ann Evans and probably built Greenmeadow Mansion on Pantgwynlais Farm. The house was demolished in 1938 but the name lives on in the beautiful Greenmeadow Wood.

The development of Melingriffith saw a steady rise in the population of Whitchurch, until by 1900 it was nearly 5,000. St Mary's Church had been rebuilt in the 17th century but in 1885, to meet the needs of the growing community, a larger and grander Gothic building in Penlline Road became the parish church. The Nonconformists also built a rich variety of chapels and as early as 1859 there were eight churches in Whitchurch, only one of which conducted services entirely in English.

Merthyr Road in Tongwynlais, 2002. The Lewis Arms and St Michael's Church are on the left, separated by the road leading to Castell Coch.

An educational report of 1847 revealed that only 8 percent of Whitchurch children attended school. There were a few private schools in the village but in 1854 a national school was built which was closely associated with the Melingriffith Works and the Booker family. Parents paid 2d a week for each child's education but, as some Nonconformist parents did not approve of sending their children to a

church school, its responsibilities were taken over by the school board in 1884. Until Whitchurch High School was opened in 1937, those children in Whitchurch who were fortunate enough to receive a secondary education travelled to Penarth or Caerphilly.

As lord of the manor in the 19th century, the Bute family assumed responsibility for most of Whitchurch Common. Gwaun Treoda, that part of the common east of Merthyr Road, was owned by Lord Tredegar and he donated it to the parish. In 1895 the parish council tried to persuade the Marquis to make a similar gesture. Negotiations were prolonged, partly because the Butes upheld the right of gypsies to camp on the common. Not until after World War Two was the matter finally resolved to the council's satisfaction. During the war, an American hospital unit was based on the common and, to mark the warm welcome they were given by local people, they planted an avenue of trees. The plaque commemorating this gesture can still be seen.

Lord Bute was responsible for the restoration of Castell Coch which began in 1875. William Burges carried out a reconstruction that externally is almost a replica of the mediaeval castle. Inside the building, Burges allowed his imagination to run riot as he created a Victorian fantasy of symbolism and decoration. The Marquis attempted to grow grapes on the slopes below the castle but, while the first few crops were promising and 40 gallons of wine were bottled in 1877, a few bad summers led to the end of the experiment.

The 17th-century St Mary's Church before it was demolished in 1904. The foundations of the church and its cemetery can be seen in Old Church Road.

Whitchurch in 1905 from St Mary's Church. At that time, open fields lay behind the Plough Public House on the corner of Old Church Road and Merthyr Road.

Whitchurch Common after World War Two, when the trees planted by American servicemen were still only saplings.

This aerial view of Whitchurch Hospital was taken in 1948. For nearly a century, the hospital has earned a high reputation for treating people with mental illnesses.

A tranquil autumn scene, as the Glamorganshire Canal flows gently through Forest Farm Country Park.

When Whitchurch became part of the Cardiff Poor Law Union in 1834, it was a sign that ties with its neighbour were becoming closer. By the end of the 19th century, Whitchurch was receiving its water supply from the Cardiff reservoirs, gas from the Cardiff Gas Company and the district was also using the borough's bus and fire services. The Cardiff Mental Hospital was opened in 1908 after the Corporation purchased the Velindre Estate. Able to accommodate 750 patients, it was equipped with the most modern facilities to treat mental illness and soon gained a national reputation for its research into this branch of medicine. Whitchurch Hospital still cares for patients with psychiatric problems, while Velindre Hospital has become a centre for cancer research.

Parts of the parish were absorbed into Cardiff in 1898 and 1922. In 1967 Whitchurch became a suburb of the city and the addition of Tongwynlais followed seven years later. Amid the urbanisation of the 20th century, there are still delightful walks in the area. The last remaining stretch of the Glamorganshire Canal winds its way through a nature reserve at Forest Farm Country Park. At Tongwynlais, the thickly wooded green belt surrounding Castell Coch is another area of outstanding beauty, reviving memories of those days when Welsh and Norman battled for supremacy in this part of Wales.

Further Reading:

Chappell, E.L. *Old Whitchurch*, Merton Priory Press, 1994

Thomas, H.M. *Whitchurch, A Brief History*, D. Brown & Sons, 1982

INDEX

Printed in Great Britain
by Amazon